The Story of
John J. Audubon

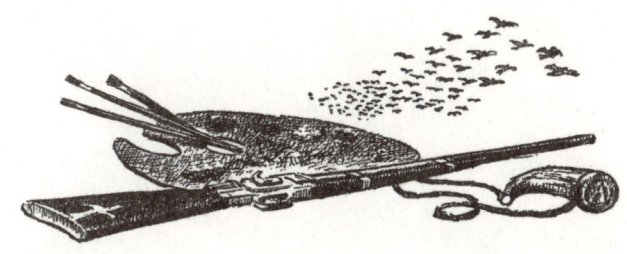

By JOAN HOWARD

Illustrated by FEDERICO CASTELLON

Originally published in 1954

Cover illustration by Ollie Cuthbertson
Cover design by Robin Fight
© 2021 Jenny Phillips
goodandbeautiful.com

CONTENTS

1. There is a Mystery Here! 1
2. More Mystery and a Promise 11
3. Trouble for Fougère 17
4. Sailors are Born, Not Made 26
5. More than One Kind of Artist 35
6. Springtime in a New World 44
7. A Gay Young Blade 52
8. John James Makes a Promise 61
9. The New Partner 71
10. Mr. and Mrs. Audubon Go West 81
11. A New World for Lucy 88
12. The Partnership Ends 96
13. A Horse Named Barro 103
14. A Cloud with a Silver Lining 111
15. Success at Last 121
16. Minnie's Land 128
17. Epilogue 133

Once these people had been the rich nobles of France

CHAPTER ONE

THERE IS A MYSTERY HERE!

It was a cold bleak day, the seventh of March, 1794. The sky hung gray as lead over the little French harbor city of Nantes. It was a frightening day, too, for an angry mob milled through the narrow streets.

Ragged women and men wearing long red caps were yelling and pushing. They jeered at other men and women who had been herded into carts that clattered over the bumpy cobblestones.

"Down with them! Kill the aristocrats!" the mob kept screaming, over and over again.

Through a shuttered window overlooking the street called the *Rue de Crébillon*, a pale boy peered out at the angry crowd. He shivered when he saw the carts full of aristocrats. Once, those people had been the rich nobles of France, but now they were prisoners. Their elegant silk and satin clothes were all torn and spattered with mud.

Standing on tiptoe beside the boy at the window, a small girl plucked at his sleeve.

"Do move your arm, Fougère!" she demanded impatiently. "You take up all the room. I want to see, too!"

But Fougère only twisted around so that he blocked her view even more completely.

"No, don't look, Rosa!" he told her. "They are horrible people, the ones who are fighting and screaming."

The room was growing dusky in the twilight. Across at the other side of it, close to the fire, sat plump Madame Audubon. When she heard the children talking, her knitting needles abruptly stopped their clicking.

"Both of you come away from that window this instant!" she commanded. "Fougère, I have told you before not to stand there."

"But it is so dark in here," the boy protested. "I wanted to watch the seagulls that fly up above the river. Some of them look as if they weren't moving their wings at all. They sit on the wind and ride on it. I wish I knew how they do that."

Whenever he saw a bird, Fougère was apt to forget everything else. He thought birds were the most exciting creatures in the whole world.

"You will have other days to watch seagulls," Madame Audubon said. Then she sighed. "It *is* dark," she admitted. "If I had to see what I knit, these stockings would never be finished for you, Fougère. But in times like these, it is safer not to show a light until the Captain comes home."

"But, *Maman*, why is it safer to sit in the dark?" small Rosa wanted to know.

"We do not want to attract the notice of that crowd," Madame explained. "Some of them might take it into their heads to break in here."

"I don't see why they should," Rosa argued. "We've never done them any harm."

"Of course we haven't. But sometimes when people get too excited, they seem to lose all the wits the good God gave them. Come over here, my dears, where you can see a little by the firelight. I want you to wind me another ball of wool."

"Yes, Madame," said Fougère. He turned away from the window. Rosa followed him across the room.

"Yes, *Maman*," Madame Audubon corrected him. She patted his shoulder when he sat down on the hassock near her feet. "Don't you remember, you are always to call me *Maman*?"

"Yes, *Maman*," said Fougère.

He was very fond of Madame Audubon, who was always so kind to him, but she was not his own mother. Fougère wished he could remember who his real mother was.

Rosa was not his real sister, either, but he loved her as much as if she were.

Both Fougère and Rosa had been told to say, if anyone should ask them questions, that Captain Audubon had brought them home in his ship from the West Indies. It might be true, but Fougère could hardly believe it.

The Captain had told them stories about the island of Santo Domingo: how its mountain seemed to rise like a green splendor out of the blue sea, how tall sugar cane grew golden around the base of the mountain and almost down to the seashore, and how bright birds had flitted among the trees—birds with purple and green feathers and topknots of red and yellow.

Fougère did not see how he could have completely forgotten a tall mountain and a long sea voyage. And he felt quite sure he would never, never have forgotten those wonderful birds.

He did remember one bright green bird that had lived in this house when first he came here. But he was not sure when that was. It might have been when he was very little, or only two or three years ago.

The bird was a pet that Captain Audubon had brought back to his wife from one of his voyages. Fougère had loved it dearly. He used to talk to it by the hour, and he laughed out loud when it answered him. For the bird was a parrot, and it spoke quite a lot of French words.

"*Du pain!*" the parrot shrieked one morning when Fougère took the cloth cover off its cage. "*Du pain pour pauvre Mignonne!*"

That meant "Bread! Bread for poor Mignonne!"

Fougère laughed. "I will feed you soon," he promised, "as soon as I have my own breakfast."

But the parrot kept on shrieking for bread until it angered another of Madame Audubon's pets. This was quite a large monkey. And the monkey reached into the cage and shook the bird until it fell dead.

"Don't hurt Mignonne!" Fougère had screamed, but he was too late to save the poor parrot. It was a long time before Madame Audubon was able to quiet Fougère's sobs. At last, they gave the parrot a fine funeral in the garden. But the boy never forgot Mignonne. And he was sure he would never have forgotten other birds like her.

Fougère sat now with the wool looped over his hands while Rosa solemnly wound it into a rather untidy ball. He stared into the fire, wondering why on earth he had such a poor memory for places and faces, for almost everything except birds.

In the flickering flames he began to see bits of scenes—something like a jigsaw puzzle that does not make a picture until all the pieces have been set in their proper places. Fougère did not think of it that way, for jigsaw puzzles had not yet been invented, but there were so many little broken pictures in his head that never seemed to fit with anything else.

There was the lady who was so different from stout Madame Audubon. She was much younger and prettier. She wore wide satin skirts. Her curls were powdered white and piled high on a small, proud head. Was that lady his own mother? Fougère did not know.

Then there was a big house as beautiful as a palace. It had tall, clipped hedges laid out in a maze that a little boy could really get lost in. And there was a garden, sunny and bright with rose trees. Was the child who chased a hoop along the sandy path among the flower beds Fougère himself? He did not know that either.

Other pieces of the puzzle were so dark that Fougère felt almost frightened when he tried to make them out, like a ride through a stormy night in a lurching, stuffy carriage with thunder and lightning crackling all around it. Fougère did not know why the carriage had been shut up so tightly. Perhaps it was because of the storm. Or it might have been because of danger from the horsemen who could be heard galloping close by.

Fougère wondered if the pictures he saw in the fire were pictures of things that had really happened to him. Or were they only daydreams that came into his head because of stories he had heard in these troubled times? He could never be sure.

He only knew that sometime in the past there had been somebody telling him he must forget things he had seen. No one said *why* he must forget, only that he must do it. And so Fougère had forgotten—almost.

Afterward, there were other things—things he had to remember. But they were quite different. And kind Madame Audubon kept reminding him of them. Her voice broke into his thoughts, and he realized that she was reminding him of one of them now.

"... and you must remember, Fougère, never to call people horrible as you did a few minutes ago."

"But, Madame—*Maman*—they *are* horrible when they are cruel!"

"Most of them don't mean to be cruel, my dear," Madame said. "We must never forget they are citizens as we are

He remembered a ride through a stormy night

ourselves. Everybody in France, whether he was high or low before this Revolution started, is now a plain citizen."

"I don't understand all about this Revolution," Fougère said, still watching the fire.

"Who does? It is not simple," Madame admitted. "You have heard the Captain tell about the American Revolution in which he fought under our gallant Marquis de Lafayette. That Revolution began because American colonists did not want to go on being ruled by the King of England. Here, it was our own King Louis who had angered many of his people. And Queen Marie Antoinette angered them even more."

"Did we have this French Revolution, and all the fighting, only because the people hated the King and Queen?" Fougère asked in astonishment.

"Of course not. But times were bad, with not enough work or food for the poor. Hungry people are angry people, and nobody can blame them for that. These hungry people saw the aristocrats and the nobles at the King's court wasting money and food. They decided that they would not be ruled any longer by such an extravagant king. They wanted France to become a republic. So riots broke out, first in Paris and then all over the country.

"Soon a civil war was raging between the royalists, who were on the King's side, and the republicans. The republicans won, and the King and Queen were put in prison. Their little son, the *Dauphin* Louis Charles, was taken away from them. And after a while, the King and Queen were both killed."

"Do the republicans kill all aristocrats?" Fougère asked.

"Many have died," Madame admitted sadly. "But some aristocrats escaped to other countries, even as far away as

America. Others went into hiding. But they are arrested when they are found, like those poor souls you saw today."

"What has become of their children?" Rosa wanted to know. "Do the republicans kill boys and girls, too?"

"Sometimes they do, I'm afraid. But a great many boys and girls have been smuggled away to safety by faithful servants. Some of the children of aristocrats have been adopted by republican families."

"What has become of the Prince, Louis Charles?" Rosa asked.

"He is supposed to be very ill, and some say he is dying, in a prison in Paris called the Temple," Madame Audubon told them. "But most people do not believe that the boy in prison is the *Dauphin* at all. They think the rightful prince was smuggled out long ago, and another boy was put in his place. There are many different ideas about where the *Dauphin* is now. I have heard people say he may be in England, or in Germany, or in Austria, or even in America. Other folks whisper that he is still right here in France."

"The poor little Prince." There were tears in Rosa's eyes. "How old is he, *Maman*?"

"I think he is the same age as I am," Fougère said, almost in a whisper. "Nine years old. Am I right, *Maman*?"

"Yes," Madame said. "You are right, Fougère."

CHAPTER TWO

MORE MYSTERY AND A PROMISE

The excitable crowd had long since gone its noisy way. The street was dark and silent. But Madame Audubon and the two children sat by the fire until a door banged. Captain Audubon blew into the house like one of his own sea winds.

"Give us light!" he shouted. "I've brought news."

Fougère jumped up to get a rushlight spill from a blue jar on the hearth. He held it to the flames. He lighted tapers in the branched candlestick on the mantel shelf. Then he circled the room, touching the candles in the shining brass wall sconces. The house took on a new, warm life.

Any room looked and sounded more alive when Captain Audubon came into it. He was so very much alive himself.

He and Fougère were as different from one another as if they had come from different worlds. Where Fougère was slim and fair, and tall for his years, Captain Audubon was stocky and bowlegged. Wind had burned his face to a color that almost matched his red hair. Fougère moved with quiet grace, while the Captain had a sailor's rolling walk and devil-may-care air.

Captain Audubon was a fine seaman, and his voyages were full of adventures that made good stories to tell Fougère and Rosa. Those were days when pirates prowled the high seas looking for trading vessels like his, and many a pirate had the Captain outrun and outfought. He had never lost a ship or a cargo to them.

Now he pulled a roll of parchment from his coat and waved it in front of his wife.

"See, *Maman*! The adoption papers for our children, all according to law and properly signed."

The Captain had begun calling Madame Audubon "*Maman*" when he first brought Fougère home. As if it might be a reminder to the boy to call her "*Maman*" also.

"Now, that is fine," Madame approved. Then her eyes grew anxious. "What did you tell those officials?"

"You need have no fears," said the Captain, striding around the room as if he were walking his quarterdeck. "I was tactful with them. I was wily as the fox."

"I hope so," said Madame Audubon, rather doubtfully. It was hard for her to imagine her bluff husband behaving wily as a fox. "These days one cannot afford to be outspoken. What did you say about Fougère's mother?"

"Ah, I did not set down a mother's name at all. I simply said she had lived in America. The word, America, covers a lot of territory, my dear. It could be Santo Domingo, where Rosa's mother died, or the United States, or even Louisiana, where there are many French people, even if it does belong to Spain right now. And as for the date of Fougère's birth, I gave it as April 22nd, 1785."

"I think you were wise," his wife agreed. "That is close enough. Perhaps someday we can tell Fougère all the facts."

"Someday, possibly, but not now. A little mystery is better than a lot of trouble, both for him and for us."

Rosa had lost interest in all this talk about adoption. It did not mean anything to her. It did not make much more sense to Fougère, though he was trying to understand.

"Come on, Fougère, draw me a picture," Rosa demanded impatiently. "Draw me the seagull sitting on the wind. You didn't give me a chance to look at him."

So Fougère went over to a corner and opened up the small sea chest the Captain had given him. It was brass-bound and had rope handles. Out of it he took his dearest treasures: three black crayons and a block of paper he used as a drawing pad.

With the pad propped on his knee, Fougère closed his eyes for a moment. He wanted to see again how the seagulls had looked when they rode the wind with motionless wings. When he opened his eyes, his crayon moved over the paper.

Rosa was soon breathing down Fougère's neck as she leaned over to watch. "It is wonderful, Fougère! Exactly like a bird."

But Fougère was not so easily satisfied.

"No, it is bad! Terrible! Inside my head I have it right. Then I put it down on paper all wrong, as stiff as if it were made of sticks and stones instead of bones and feathers."

"Here, let me see it," the Captain said. He inspected the seagull closely and carefully. "It is better than the last one you drew, Fougère. Of course, there is a list to starboard. And perhaps the tail is a little loose, something like an unshipped rudder."

Fougère had to laugh at that. He felt better then. "Someday I will get it *exactly* right. I want to draw every kind of bird there is in the whole world."

"Well, you can begin on the pigeons at La Gerbetière next week," Captain Audubon said. "I am going to send you children and *Maman* to our country house. There is less fighting there, and I have to go on another voyage. Crops were bad again last year, so hungry people need the food I can bring back."

"But, Captain—Papa," Fougère spoke with a little hesitation, "is it the republican government you go on a mission for? Are you a republican, too?"

"We are all republicans in this country nowadays. You must remember that always, Fougère." The Captain seemed to be warning the boy in almost the same words his wife had used earlier. "As for me, it is not for *any* government that I go. Governments are only men sitting in a big building telling other men what to do. It is my country

Fougère had to laugh at that

that needs my help—and my countrymen who are hungry. I have fought for France in the past, and I shall fight for France any time I am needed."

"Yes," said Fougère. "I think I feel that way, too, about France."

"At La Gerbetière, can I take my doll to play out of doors?" Rosa broke in.

"As soon as the weather turns warm enough," Madame Audubon assured her.

"How many kinds of birds are there at La Gerbetière?" Fougère was asking the question most important to him.

"Hundreds, without a doubt," the Captain said. "How would I know how many kinds there are?"

"Well, I mean to know before we come back," Fougère promised.

CHAPTER THREE

TROUBLE FOR FOUGÈRE

If Fougère did not meet every bird in France that summer, he certainly learned to know every feathered creature that nested near La Gerbetière.

He began by making friends with the pigeons in the courtyard. He liked the soft rustling noise they made, like the swish of Madame Audubon's best silk taffeta skirt. He studied their pink feet and their beady eyes. Then he tried to draw them, with the feathered ruffs raised around their gleaming necks. But he could not make the feathers lie properly in his picture.

At night, Fougère stayed awake as long as he could. He leaned on his windowsill watching for the owl that slept in the gray stone church tower all day.

"Hoo-o-o! Hoo-o-o!" the owl cried as it flew across the silvery path of moonlight.

In her bedroom next to Fougère's, Rosa heard it and was frightened. She covered her head with the quilt.

Fougère shivered, too, at the ghostly sound. But he shivered with pleasure. He held his breath waiting to hear it again.

"Fougère, won't you forget your old birds and play with me?" Rosa asked him one morning.

"No," said Fougère. "But if you promise to walk quietly and not say a word, I'll take you to the woods to see birds."

That was not Rosa's idea of fun. So she found another little girl to play dolls with her. And Fougère went off by himself. He stumbled along, not looking where he was going, because his head was tilted back to watch a skylark spiraling up into the golden air. The notes of its song were like a rain of melody falling from the summer sky.

Every day Fougère wandered farther afield. Madame Audubon always packed a little lunch in a basket for him. Toward sunset he came back, always with the basket filled with curious stones and mosses, with birds' eggs and feathers. The day he found a dead bluebird, he brought that back with him, too. He set it up against a board in his room and began drawing it.

Fougère still had that bluebird when Madame told the children they were moving back to Nantes. Summer was over. Madame was anxious to get home and see to a good housecleaning before cold weather set in.

"And I must see about a school for you, Fougère," she said. "I promised the Captain I would do that as soon as the city was safe. Now, thanks be to God, the dreadful reign of terror is over in Nantes. The citizens are sick of bloodshed. They demand law and order from their new government now."

"Does that mean that aristocrats are safe again?" Fougère wanted to know. "Can they live just like anybody else now?"

Madame Audubon stopped a moment to think before she answered that question.

"No, the aristocrats still in France must stay hidden. It is safer so. But that, my dear little son, need not concern you. In Nantes, you and Rosa shall be quite safe, I promise you."

Shortly after a soft pink sunrise, Madame and the children climbed into a coach for the drive back to the city. Rosa sat beside Madame, with Fougère opposite them. His own little *portmanteau* was under his feet.

As they rolled along, leaving a cloud of dust behind, a horrid stench spread through the coach. Madame fumbled in her reticule to find her spiced pomander ball. Rosa held her nose.

"What on earth is that terrible smell?" Rosa asked.

"Yes, what is it?" Madame added. "Fougère, what do you have in your *portmanteau*?"

"I'm afraid, *Maman*, it is my bluebird. It is quite dead, you see."

"I am inclined to believe you," declared Madame. "Tell the driver to pull up so we can get rid of it."

"Oh, please, no, *Maman*!" Fougère cried in alarm. "I have almost finished drawing it. If I throw away my model, my picture will be spoiled entirely. Besides, it has such pretty blue wings—even yet."

Madame Audubon started to draw a deep breath. Quickly she thought better of it and put the pomander to her nose again. She knew she ought to be strict, but she could never deny Fougère anything he asked.

"Very well, then," she said. "But we must have the windows open the whole way, and we shall all get very dusty."

"I like to have them open," Fougère said happily. "Now I can watch for that mavis I heard whistling a minute ago."

They found the city quiet, and in a few days Madame sent Fougère off to school. That he did not like at all. He hated sitting at a desk in an ugly room when he wanted to be outdoors. The schoolmaster was a long gloomy man who told his pupils a great many dull facts. He always had a cold in his head that kept him sneezing and snuffling.

Fougère only heard half what his teacher said. Less than half made any sense to him. He was especially bad at arithmetic and never could make a sum come out right. One morning when the teacher came down the aisle to inspect the work on Fougère's slate, he saw a drawing of himself looking exactly like a stork. The rest of that day, Fougère had to stand in the corner.

Madame wanted to make up to Fougère for the dull hours in school. She arranged for him to buy anything he wanted at the pastry shop and the toy store and charge his purchases to her.

Not one of Fougère's schoolmates was allowed to do that. He soon found himself popular with boys who hoped for sugar drops and sweet cakes called *petit fours*. Then the other pupils discovered that Fougère was always ready to exchange a brand-new spinning top or ball for any unusual feather or bird's egg. That was the beginning of a brisk trading that went on every recess time.

"It is most important that you learn how to behave like a great gentleman," Madame told Fougère. She arranged for him to have private tutors for music and dancing and fencing lessons.

Fougère quite enjoyed those lessons when they did not interrupt his visits to the birds. He was naturally quick and graceful. It was easy for him to learn all the fashionable dances, the *pavane* and *gavotte* and *minuet*. In fencing, he handled a sword like one born to it. He began to play the violin and flute and flageolet.

The little flageolet he liked best of all. It was rather like a whistle, small enough to be carried in his pocket.

"I can take it to the woods and practice the songs of the birds," he said.

As often as he could, he escaped from the small city, with his flageolet in his pocket. He watched the flight of swallows over the sparkling waters of the Loire River. He followed his own secret paths through fields and woods where no one saw him except the birds and sometimes a field mouse or rabbit.

In Madame Audubon's eyes he could do no wrong. "My Fougère is the handsomest young gentleman in all France," she boasted to her neighbors.

"The airs that woman gives herself," one woman whispered to another. "You would think the boy was a prince, to hear her talk."

There is no doubt that Fougère was spoiled. Poor Madame Audubon had no idea she was storing up trouble for him in the future. The Captain was not at home to warn her.

Then one day when Fougère was fourteen years old, Captain Audubon blew into the house like a strong salt breeze. He was in uniform, for he now held a commission in the French Navy.

"I'm just back from Plymouth," he told his family when they sat down to supper.

"Where is Plymouth, Papa?" Fougère asked.

The Captain was so startled that he choked on a crust of bread. "Do you mean to say you haven't learned that much geography in school? Plymouth is in England, and a fine port, too."

"How horrid for you to have to go there," Fougère said. "I hate Englishmen. They are always fighting France."

The Captain laughed. "They might say that Frenchmen are always fighting England. You will change these fire-eating notions as you grow older. I have fought the English many times. I have been their prisoner. But I have found many fine men among them, and I've left good friends in Plymouth."

"Well, I refuse to know any Englishmen, ever," Fougère said. He passed his plate for a second helping of omelet.

"Now I shall look over your lesson books," the Captain told the children after supper. "Ladies first. Let us see what Rosa has been doing."

He inspected Rosa's copybook. "Very nice and neat," he told her. "What progress do you make on the harpsichord?"

While Rosa played a tinkling minuet on the rosewood spinet, Fougère watched the candlelight sparkling on the glass prisms of the chandelier. He tried not to think about his turn coming next. Madame's knitting needles were idle, and she looked anxious.

"Now, Fougère, what have you to show me?" the Captain said when he had clapped his approval of Rosa's tune.

"Will you come upstairs to see, Papa?"

Fougère led the way to his own room, followed by his father, Madame, and Rosa.

"Ugh, smells again!" Rosa said when he opened the door.

Eggshells of every size had been blown out and hung on threads from bedposts and door latch. Moss and flowers and branches littered the table and chairs and bureau. Old nests were stuffed into every nook that would hold them. And there were birds! Some that had been stuffed. Others that ought to have been stuffed—or buried.

The Captain cleared his throat. "Very interesting, but . . ."

Quickly, Fougère began pulling drawings out of a drawer. He spread them on the floor and propped them against the walls.

"Do you like this green woodpecker, Papa? I traded my penknife for that bird. This hoopoe isn't very good, but the spotted sandpiper is better, don't you think? I shot that wild duck myself. I'm a good shot now. I can put a bullet through a tossed cork at twenty-five paces, you must know."

TROUBLE FOR FOUGÈRE

At last Fougère had to stop talking for lack of breath. The Captain broke in. "Now I will see your lesson books."

"Remember, the boy had measles only a few weeks ago," Madame hurried to remind her husband.

"I will inspect the books he did before he was ill, then."

So the copybooks had to be brought out. Even Fougère knew they were a disgrace, untidy and full of mistakes. He hung his head and waited for his scolding. It did not come.

The Captain simply walked out of the room, humming the minuet tune that Rosa had been playing downstairs. Madame Audubon hurried after him.

"I thought you would catch it this time," Rosa told her brother when they were alone.

"So did I," Fougère admitted. "But I have a feeling, Rosa, that this may be worse."

CHAPTER FOUR

SAILORS ARE BORN, NOT MADE

The earliest birds were exchanging the news as they hunted for their breakfast worms when Madame Audubon woke Fougère the next morning.

"Get up quickly, my dear. You are going on a trip."

Fougère sat up and yawned widely. "Where?"

"That your father will have to tell you," said Madame. Her eyes were red, as if she had been crying. "I'll pack for you."

"Oh, may I take the chaffinch eggs I found yesterday? I think they are quite fresh. I'll wrap them in cotton so they won't break in the trunk."

"No, Fougère. Nothing is to go but your clothes and violin."

Fougère still knew nothing more when Madame and Rosa said goodbye at the gate where the carriage waited. Hugging Fougère, Madame managed to drop a little purse of coins into his pocket.

The country roads were bumpy, and the carriage jolted until Fougère felt giddy and sick. In spite of the lurching, Captain Audubon pulled out of his pocket a leather-bound book and began to read.

Fougère knew this meant he was not to talk. He tried to look for birds in the trees they swept past, but his heart was not in it. He felt sure his old carefree life was at an end.

He wondered if they were going to the great city of Paris. Years ago, he remembered, *Maman* had told him about a little boy who was imprisoned there in the Temple. Since then, there had been an official announcement that the boy was dead. Some people believed it was the *Dauphin* who had died. Others believed that Louis Charles was still living somewhere in hiding.

"If he is alive, he must be just my age," Fougère thought, "and he is really the rightful King Louis the Seventeenth of France."

There were questions Fougère wanted to ask his father about that boy. But he did not dare do it now.

Behind his book, Captain Audubon was not happy either. He was only using it as a screen against questions he did not want to answer. He was sure the time had come when Fougère had to have some real discipline.

For four days they traveled, most of the time in silence. They stopped for meals at wayside inns. They paused to change horses. They slept in strange bedrooms. At last the carriage rolled through the gate of Rochefort, the seaport town that was France's chief naval base. The carriage stopped before a little house.

With a big brass key, Captain Audubon unlocked the door. The coachman brought in Fougère's trunk, and the boy carried his violin case.

When the captain threw open the shutters to let in the sunlight, Fougère looked around. He could see at once that his comfortable mother had never had any hand in settling this house of his father's. It was tidy and shipshape, but there was no coziness about it.

The model of a man-of-war stood on the mantel. The walls were covered with maps and yellowing charts of coastal waters. The Captain set the ship's clock going by his big pocket watch. He motioned for Fougère to sit down.

"Now, my son, here we can talk without any women to interfere in men's affairs. The whole French Navy is in port, so we are safe."

Fougère wondered if his father was making a joke. Did he mean it would take the French Navy to defend him

against gentle *Maman*? He could not make it out, and the Captain was talking.

"I have neglected you, and they were making a regular mollycoddle out of you. But I blame only myself. Now, you are going to what I consider the best school in France. It is a school where you will learn to become an officer in the Navy. Of course there will be periods every day for pleasures with your classmates, but the rest of your hours must be employed in work."

"Am I to live here with you, Papa?" Fougère asked doubtfully.

"No, you will live in barracks," the Captain said. "But today is ours to spend together. I have business at the docks, but if you want to see the ships of war and walk along the wall, you may come with me."

Fougère already had one virtue that would always stand by him when life proved hard. He never whined about what could not be helped. So he stood up now and smiled.

"There is one more matter to be settled before we go out," the Captain said. "I feel it wiser for you now to give up the name of Fougère. You are beginning a new life here at Rochefort, and you will commence it with a new name. You shall be called Jean Jacques Audubon, named after me."

"I am honored to have your name," Fougère said politely.

This sudden change of name was the most puzzling part of the whole mysterious trip. Fougère knew his father must have a good reason for what he was doing, but he could not guess what it was.

"Jean Jacques Audubon," the Captain repeated. "You might add LaForêt, if that name pleases you."

"Oh, it does, Papa! It means forest, and you know I love the woods."

"I do know," said the Captain. "But after this you will not love them too much to do your duty, eh?"

"No, Papa." Fougère, who had become Jean Jacques LaForêt Audubon, tried to keep the doubt out of his voice. He had no desire to become an officer in the Navy. Never would a ship have as much meaning for him as any bird. Never would he be able to love the sea as he loved deep woods.

Sunshine tipped the waves that day, and a stiff breeze kept the flags snapping. In the ship basin, masts stood as thick as the trees along the banks of the Loire. The boy and his father stepped over coils of tarred rope. They dodged barrels being trundled to the wharf for loading. Now and again the Captain halted to present his son to some officer, very fine in sash and cocked hat, gold lace, and sword.

"Is this another Audubon to carry on your fine work at sea?" one of them asked.

For all his worry, Jean Jacques LaForêt Audubon felt it was good to be proud of one's father.

Before the guns in the fort fired the sunset salute, he had been enrolled in the naval school and put into uniform. He was introduced to a young officer named Gabriel Loyen du Puigaudeau. The officer looked him over as if he did not think much of the boy inside the new clothes.

"Straighten your shoulders! Pull your chin in! Eyes front!" he roared at this youngest cadet.

Jean Jacques had never been spoken to like that in his life. He expected his father to shout down such rudeness. But the Captain only grinned at the young officer.

"That's the way!" he approved. "I expect you to pull this boy into shape."

Jean Jacques felt that Gabriel Loyen du Puigaudeau was his enemy, and he hated him. Even more, he detested the dull work he had to do in the fortress and on the training ship. He loathed the parade ground. There were cockroaches in the barracks. He did not want to study them, as he wanted to study every insect that lived outdoors.

One frosty January morning, the world shone like a cobwebbed fairyland. Jean Jacques felt he could not bear to stay inside another instant. But it was his old enemy Arithmetic that finally pushed him into rebellion.

He stared at a column of figures that seemed to be grinning at him just like that haughty Puigaudeau. Suddenly he noticed that he was alone in the room.

He jumped up from his desk and whisked across to the window. Without thinking twice, he was over the sill and dropping to the ground. Then he ran, skimming among the bushes, close to the ground like a chimney swallow.

Jean Jacques had not planned his escape. His only hope was to get away to deep forest where he might hunt to feed himself. But it was not to be. As he darted through the garden, a hand reached out from the bushes and snatched him back by the scruff of his neck. A corporal, whom he had always found friendly before, marched him back as a deserter.

Within the hour, Cadet Jean Jacques Audubon was sitting in the smelly darkness of the hold in the prison ship. He had been a fool. Now he had to pay for it.

"Already you disgrace your father's honored name," said Gabriel du Puigaudeau, who had sent him there.

The boy thought about those words for hours as he cringed away from the other prisoners. Most of them were rough men who had already spent much time in jails. The

moldy food he was given turned his stomach. The drinking water was filthy. He would never forget things he saw in that place of punishment.

But most of all he would never forget the moment when he was called up on deck to face his father. Captain Audubon had come back from sea duty when he heard of his son's disgrace. He did not scold Jean Jacques. He took him home for a bath. Then he sent him back to the Academy in a clean uniform.

Jean Jacques spent a whole year more in that school, and he hated every day of it. But at last the year ended, and he and his father traveled back to Nantes by coach. As they left the coach, Jean Jacques swaggered a little when street urchins admired his uniform. Rosa thought her big brother

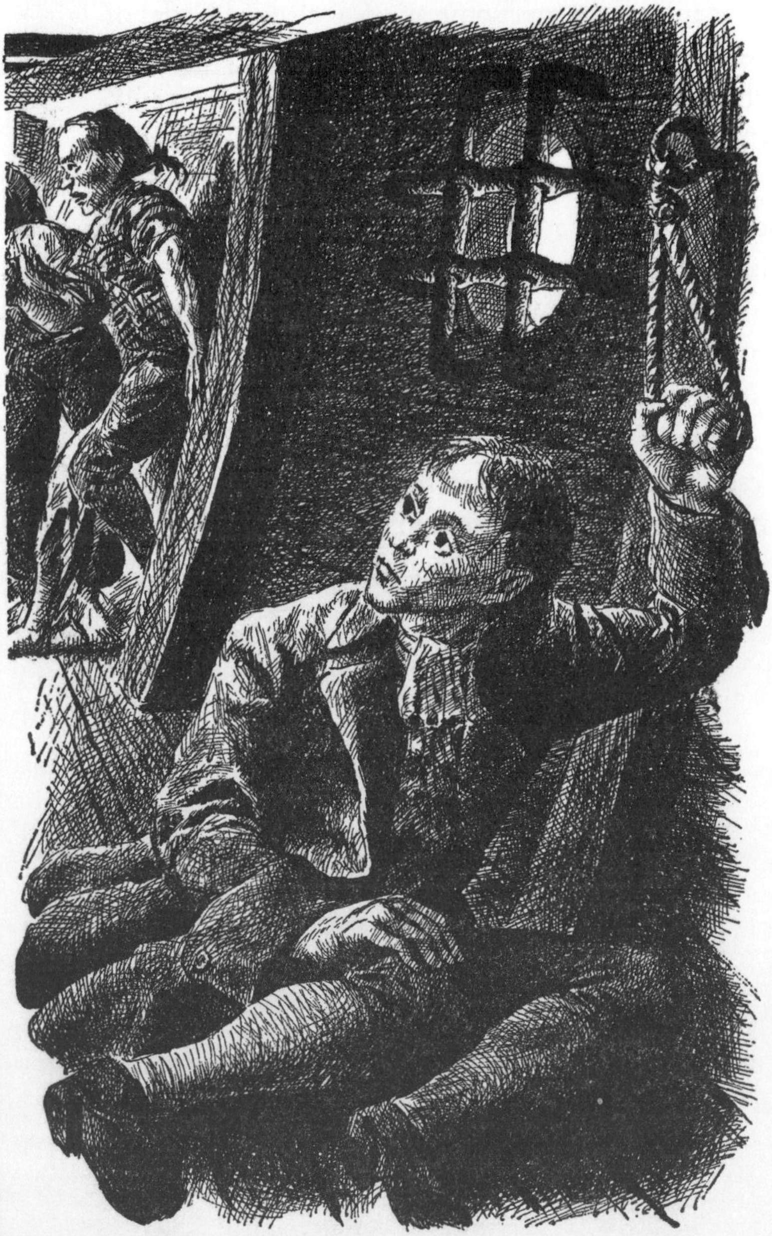

looked wonderfully handsome as a full-fledged Cadet of the French Navy.

"Oh, my Fougère, it has been so long since you went away," sobbed Madame.

"Yes, *Maman*, I think so, too. But, you must know, my name is no longer Fougère. It is now Jean Jacques LaForêt Audubon. I'd like you to call me LaForêt."

An hour later, Madame Audubon was telling her husband that their boy was the handsomest cadet in the world. He had the finest manners. "He can do anything. I have always said so. See how he honors the uniform."

"Yes, my dear," the Captain said. "But it takes more than a uniform and charming manners to make a naval officer. Sailors are born, not made. I'm afraid that our boy was not born to be a sailor."

CHAPTER FIVE

MORE THAN ONE KIND OF ARTIST

Before many days were out, Captain Audubon knew that he was right. Jean Jacques would never be a sailor. He did not even want to talk about ships.

At school he had dreamed of his own room here at home as a sort of heaven waiting for him. But it had proved a big disappointment. Carpet beetles had chewed up his stuffed owl. The eggshells had been broken. A housecleaning had swept out the old nests and feathers. But Madame had carefully tied up his portfolio and put it away for him.

His heart beat hard when he tugged at the green tape. He threw back the cover and pulled out his drawings. Then he felt as if somebody had thrown cold water in his face. Surely those pictures were not his! They were only a child's scribblings.

"Sticks!" Jean Jacques told himself furiously. "How could I have thought I was drawing real birds when I did them?"

Jean Jacques made himself look at every one of the drawings. Woodpeckers and sandpipers, willow warblers and chaffinches. There were more than a hundred pictures. One after another, he judged them and tore them into shreds. At last only a heap of paper scraps littered the floor.

"There!" he said. "Now I am ready to start again. But this time I have to learn how to do it right."

The Captain was working on his account books when Jean Jacques rushed into his study.

"Father," he said, "I have to take lessons. I must learn to draw properly."

This past year at the Academy, he had given up calling the Captain "Papa." "Father" was the proper word for a young man to use. At almost sixteen, he was feeling very grown up.

"So, after all, this bird drawing is still in your mind, is it?" The Captain did not sound really surprised to hear it.

"Yes, Father. What would you have done when you were my age if anybody had tried to keep you off a ship? What if they said you had to work at a counting-house desk or maybe become a schoolmaster?"

"They'd not have dared!" the Captain roared in his quarter-deck voice.

Then he caught sight of the grin on his son's face. He turned red, and his voice died away in a rumble.

"I see your point, my boy," he admitted. "But if you must be an artist, I want you to be a good one. I shall send you to Paris to study with Jacques Louis David. Monsieur David is considered the greatest painter in all France."

"Is he an artist of birds, Father?"

"I suppose so." The Captain sounded surprised at such a question. "Any artist can paint birds, surely. M. David came all the way from Paris to paint the portrait of our mayor. The picture is enormous and very like the mayor, too."

Jean Jacques was not sure this great M. David was a fine bird painter just because he could do an enormous likeness of the Mayor of Nantes. He had seen the mayor, and he was not at all like a bird. He was more like a donkey, perhaps, except for the ears.

"I don't know what your poor *Maman* is going to say about all this," the Captain said. "Paris is a very big city, and sometimes it is both wicked and dangerous. Your *Maman* worries when you are not right under her eye, you know."

"Yes, Father, I know."

"Well, no matter, I will talk to her." The Captain sighed. "And you take care to keep out of scrapes, for I shan't be there to get you out of them. Stay out of debt, and don't starve yourself to buy stuffed birds." He began to sharpen his quill pen to write a letter to M. David.

"Yes, Father." Jean Jacques felt rather choked. "You are good to me, and after I disgraced you at Rochefort that time."

"That is over, and we do not speak of it," the Captain said gruffly. "You are a good boy, too. It is only that I do not understand you, perhaps."

Some time later Jean Jacques said goodbye to his family and set off by coach for Paris. His *portmanteau* was strapped on the outside because his legs were too long now for him to ride with it under his feet.

Paris looked enormous to the boy from Nantes, with miles of winding streets to get lost in. He was amazed when he reached the building called the Louvre that was to be his home and school.

The Louvre was already hundreds of years old. It had been a royal fort and then a palace. Now it held galleries full of some of the most famous paintings in the world. A few fine artists like M. David lived there and gave lessons in their studios. Their pupils occupied rooms which were reached by a narrow spiral staircase.

"If you're the new pupil, go to the very top," a cross old man told Jean Jacques. "You'll know when you reach there, from the noise those young devils make. And carry your own trunk."

Jean Jacques balanced the *portmanteau* on one shoulder and carried his violin in his other hand. Around and around those winding steps he climbed, higher than he had known one could go inside a building. The trunk grew heavier. He was breathing in short gasps when at last he was right up under the roof.

He went into a room with rows of cot beds and a great deal of litter about. A dozen young men stopped gabbling to stare at him. Most of them were a good deal older than he.

"Now they send us babies," one said with a laugh. "From

the country, too, to judge by his clothes."

Jean Jacques let his trunk slide to the floor. He had a quick temper, and he was ready to teach this fellow a lesson in manners.

"Don't mind them. Every newcomer has to put up with the same thing." The young man who spoke was tall and homely. But he had a quick, lopsided smile that won an answering grin from Jean Jacques. "Stow your *portmanteau* under the bed next to mine, that one directly under the window. You can get a fine view of the chimney pots of Paris. And when it rains, you will also get a large drop of water on your pillow. My name is Pierre, by the way. Pierre Couteau."

"I am Jean Jacques LaForêt Audubon. I shan't mind leaks."

"Listen to the babe," came a jeering voice. "Two names are not enough for this one. He has to have four."

Now that Jean Jacques had found a friend in Pierre, he paid little attention to the other students. He caught a glimpse of the view Pierre had promised him. It held him spellbound.

"Tell me about M. David, Pierre," Jean Jacques said as he sat on the edge of his cot after they blew out their candles.

"You will find him stern," said Pierre. "But there are many who think he is an excellent teacher. You'll learn more about him tomorrow. I'm too tired to talk of him now. I am going to sleep."

Jean Jacques thought that was a good idea. He was weary from the jolting of the coach for the past several days. Even a thin, hard mattress would be a luxury tonight.

There was a little scuffle in the dark close by, just before he put his head down on his pillow. He found the pillow

He went into a room with rows of cot beds

soaking wet. A fellow student had just poured a pitcher of water over his bed.

"To give you an idea what it is like when it rains."

"Well, I'm sleepy. Good night, all," Jean Jacques said. He curled up in the sopping-wet bed and slept soundly.

The next morning Jean Jacques went down the winding stairs to the studio of M. David. It was the biggest room he had ever seen. Except for the north side, which held long windows, all the walls were covered with M. David's works: enormous oil paintings showing enormous people; pictures of citizens assassinating a tyrant; and ships with banks of galley slaves chained to their oars. They all made Jean Jacques unhappy.

Except for the pupils' easels, the middle of the room was full of giants—white plaster giants that he was supposed to copy.

For half the first morning, M. David paid no attention to the new pupil standing beside an empty easel. Then he was brusque.

"Show me what you have brought in your portfolio."

"I have only two drawings, a kingfisher and a snowy owl," Jean Jacques said, opening his portfolio. "You see, I was not satisfied with my other work, so I tore it up to begin fresh."

"Tear these up, too," said the painter. "They are trash. You will not waste your time and mine on birds here." With a ruler, he touched the ear of one of the white giants. "Copy that ear until you have it perfect."

For a time Jean Jacques hoped he would be allowed to work from a model that was real to him, one of bones and feathers and delicate claws. But he was kept to copying the noses and feet and elbows of giants. He wanted to learn to use color, but only black crayon was permitted. M. David had very little interest in him and no sympathy with his dream of becoming a bird painter.

"Sheer waste of time," was his only comment to that.

"I thought art school was going to be wonderful, but here I am as bored as a beetle," Jean Jacques muttered. He stared despairingly out of the window at the pigeons strutting along the ledges of the church of St. Germain. He was homesick for his woods and river. And he felt guilty because he was wasting his father's money.

One day a very dusty boy turned up in Nantes, carrying his violin. He had walked all the way from Paris, using the last of his money to send his trunk home by coach. Madame Audubon wept over a blister on his heel and clucked over the state of his clothes.

"So now you change your mind about learning to draw," said Captain Audubon.

"I'll never do that, Father," replied Jean Jacques. "But I could not learn from M. David. We are too different. He sees big bold outlines. I like tiny details of a feather or the wrinkles on a claw."

"And you set yourself up to say this master is wrong, and you are right. Is that it?"

Jean Jacques wished he could make the Captain understand. "M. David is right, for himself. I have to be right for me, too."

Captain Audubon shook his head. It was too much for him. "We shall have to see what to do about you."

Jean Jacques had longed to draw birds when he was in Paris. Now he drew them all day and as far into the night as Madame permitted. He worked indoors and out, with watercolors and crayons. By the time the Captain had decided what to do with him, Jean Jacques had pictures of a hundred birds, all numbered in orderly fashion.

"Let me show you this." Jean Jacques held out to his parents a drawing of a thrush on her nest in the crotch of a tree. In the distance a tiny stretch of river appeared. "In the bird pictures I have seen, the artist has set the birds on stiff perches as if they were stuffed specimens in a museum. I want to make them look at home among trees and fields and flowers."

"Already you are the best bird painter in all France," Madame Audubon declared loyally.

"Oh, no, *Maman*! I am still very bad. But I mean to keep on until I am good at it, if it takes me all my life."

Affection did not blind the Captain. He saw that the pictures were far from perfect, although they were improving.

"You will soon be eighteen years old," he said. "It is time you did something besides chasing birds. I could send you across the ocean to the property I own in America—to Mill Grove in Pennsylvania."

"Is that the house you told me about, where you left the portrait General Washington gave you?" Jean Jacques asked. "I should like to see that picture."

"I will not be sending you to America to look at pictures and birds," said the Captain sternly. "America is the New World of opportunity. Failures in the Old World go there and make their fortunes. There is adventure in the very air. I myself feel it again. But I send you in my place. The future is yours, my boy."

Jean Jacques began to see that the future might be very bright. A new world would have new birds. Thousands of new birds! This time he did not tell his parents what he was thinking.

CHAPTER SIX

SPRINGTIME IN A NEW WORLD

Jean Jacques stood on a grassy knoll in front of the red stone farmhouse at Mill Grove. A new spring was coming into blossom in a world that was just as new to him.

He did not notice the stares of the farmhands coming back from plowing or bringing cows in from pasture. He did not know what an unusual sight a French boy was here, in his black satin knee breeches and fine ruffled shirt.

Cherry trees were bursting into bloom like enormous bouquets. They stood in such orderly rows that Jean Jacques could easily imagine his father planting them years ago. Captain Audubon always wanted everything, even nature, to be trim and shipshape.

More beautiful to Jean Jacques were the tumbling waters of Perkiomen Creek hurrying to spill into the Schuylkill River. Small drifts of snow still lay against the north side of the house. But here and there a marsh marigold gleamed like a tiny sun along the banks. Willow trees put out new leaves of palest green. Everywhere, and best of all to Jean Jacques, there were birds.

Hundreds of birds! Thousands of birds! Birds he had known at home and birds he had never seen before, all in full song to welcome him to Mill Grove.

"At last!" Jean Jacques told himself. "This is America the way I used to dream about it."

America had been a disappointment at first. After a tedious voyage that lasted seven weeks, he had reached New York and set out to explore the city. It seemed very crowded and bustling after sleepy Nantes. Jean Jacques spoke no English yet, and he couldn't find anybody who spoke French. He began to feel dreadfully ill. His head ached, so he could hardly find his way back to the ship.

"Will you take me back to France?" he had asked the ship's captain. "I do not think I like America."

"No wonder; you are a sick boy," the captain said.

Jean Jacques had caught yellow fever. The captain took him to some friends of his who kept a boardinghouse. These two gentle Quaker ladies nursed the boy devotedly until he was able to travel again. And when he reached Mill Grove, Friend Thomas, the Quaker farmer who was Captain Audubon's caretaker, had given him a real welcome.

Mrs. Thomas was a comfortable woman who reminded Jean Jacques of Madame Audubon. She was very well pleased to have a boy to spoil and keep house for. Almost the first thing she showed him was the picture of George Washington, which Washington himself had given Captain Audubon.

"It was presented to the good Captain after General Washington and his army defeated the British at Yorktown," she explained. "That was the great victory which ended the Revolutionary War, and Captain Audubon helped us win it. He was in command of a corvette which kept the British ships bottled up in the harbor so that none could escape. So he was given this picture."

Jean Jacques studied the portrait. The picture was too stiff to be lifelike. But he thought the great general's face was both commanding and noble. And everything else about Mill Grove charmed the boy.

"It is perfect!" Jean Jacques said, on his first day.

He found it perfect all through that golden springtime. He had his own gun and his own horse. He had a wonderful dog named Zephyr who was quick at learning tricks. He had a house that was his own home. He was the squire of broad acres and of woods full of new birds.

Soon he was dizzy from trying to count the new birds: great blue herons and the little green herons that Friend Thomas called Fly-up-the-creeks, whip-poor-wills and bobolinks, and blackbirds wearing scarlet shoulder patches. He could scarcely believe his eyes when he saw his first ruby-throated hummingbird. It looked to him as if it had flown straight out of a fairy tale.

"Thou belongs in one of these fables," he told the bird. The Thomases were teaching him to speak English. So of course he used the Quaker "thee" and "thou" as they did.

He tapped the book he carried in his pocket. It was his favorite of all books, the *Fables* of La Fontaine. In those stories, animals and birds talked with wit and wisdom.

One evening when he was passing the grist mill that gave Mill Grove its name, Jean Jacques heard a noise. It sounded like a saw being sharpened against a grindstone. He peered in the window, but nobody was there. The next time he heard the rasping noise, it was directly above his head.

A bird flew out of an old hemlock tree. It was the little Acadian owl the farmers called a saw-whet. He tried to follow it, but it was gone like a ghost in the dark. Even though its cry was different, the saw-whet reminded him of the owl in the steeple at La Gerbetière. He wondered if that owl's "Hoo-hoo!" still frightened Rosa.

Sometimes he was homesick and lonely for his family in France. But there was plenty here to keep him occupied.

Again and again he explored the high wooded banks of the Perkiomen. Once he discovered caves scooped out of limestone. He wondered whether the stream had hollowed them out, or if they were the work of ancient cave dwellers.

Exploring the largest of these caves, he found a mysterious little nest made of mud and lined with moss. The nest was empty, but Jean Jacques did not take it away.

"I think the bird is going to come back home," he said to himself. "I think I will make me a home here, too, and wait for it."

He brought his drawing pad and crayons and stored them in the cave. He found a ledge of rock exactly the right height to use as a table. Day after day, he stayed there for hours. Sometimes he sketched the scene from the mouth of the cave. Sometimes he read the *Fables*. Always he was watching for a bird to come flying across the stream, or over the budding maple trees.

On the tenth day of April, 1804, a pair of gray-white birds marked with dusky olive and yellow arrived near sunset. They looked tired as they glided into the cave. It was the phoebes come home.

"Today I shall not bother them," Jean Jacques thought. "But I will come back tomorrow. I want to know everything about them."

He had no idea that this was the date upon which he was starting to be a scientist as well as an artist and bird lover.

The phoebes' feathers looked brighter as they chased insects in the warm air next morning. As Jean Jacques moved toward the cave, the male bird flew down in front of him, snapping its bill. Its call was a trembling, rolling note. Jean Jacques did not go into the cave. Instead, he took out his flageolet and practiced the phoebe's song until he got it right.

Jean Jacques had learned to be very patient. He sat close to the cave, reading and watching, until the phoebes paid no attention to him. Little by little, he inched closer to the cave. At last he was able to slip inside and watch them at work. They added new grass and soft moss to the old nest. They gave it a fresh lining made from feathers and down. It looked like a mossy plant hung from the rock.

Six eggs were laid, white with reddish speckles at one end. By the time the eggs hatched, the parent birds knew Jean Jacques very well. They even let him slip his fingers into the nest to touch the fledglings gently.

Other pairs of phoebes built their homes in smaller caves and in the rafters of the mill. But the ones in his cave were his special friends. He spent hours sketching them. He drew them darting into the sunlit mouth of their cave. He drew them sitting in their nest or on branches in the maple trees.

"Alive and moving," he kept saying to himself. He tore up one picture after another. "I *must* get them alive and moving. What I've done are no better than jumping jacks."

He studied all the habits of the phoebes. He was certain they had come back to a home they knew.

"If I can only find some way to prove it," he said.

Very few people in those days believed that birds migrate. They thought the swallow skimming over a pond hibernated under its water like a frog. Other birds, they said, hid in belfries and hollow trees to sleep all winter.

One day Jean Jacques had a wonderful idea. He ran to the house and pulled his grandest waistcoat from the closet. It was embroidered in fine silver thread. He began ripping out the stitches.

"Has thou taken leave of thy senses, lad?" Mrs. Thomas asked.

"I don't think so," Jean Jacques told her seriously. "What I want to do is put a silver thread around the leg of each of my phoebes. I'll be careful to make it loose enough not to hurt them. Then I shall know my birds if they come back next spring."

It was such a simple plan—so simple that nobody had thought of it before. Jean Jacques would have been astonished if he could have known that, a hundred years afterward, a Bird Banding Society would be carrying on the work he had begun. People would still be studying the migration of birds. And he would not have believed anyone who told him that another society of bird lovers would be named after him—The Audubon Society of America.

Twilight was settling over the sitting room when he came in from banding the phoebes that day. The housekeeper had a message for him.

"Thou had a visitor," Mrs. Thomas said. "Mr. Bakewell. That English gentleman who has just lately bought Fatland Ford."

Fatland Ford was the mansion across the river from Mill Grove. It was an imposing house with white pillars rising two stories high. It had a walled garden and a carriage drive.

Jean Jacques scowled as he threw an applewood log on the fire. "I do not want to know any Englishmen. I do not like Englishmen. If he comes again, tell him I am not at home and that I am not likely to be at home."

Mrs. Thomas looked shocked.

"Thy manners could do with some mending, I'm thinking." It was the first time she had ever scolded him.

Jean Jacques flashed her the bright smile she could never resist. "Now, Mother Thomas, doesn't *thou* like my manners?"

"Thou can charm the birds out of the trees when thou has a mind to," the old lady admitted tartly.

Jean Jacques laughed.

"Wonderful! Charming birds out of trees is just what I want to do. But I do not want to charm Englishmen at all. Them I will leave strictly alone."

CHAPTER SEVEN

A GAY YOUNG BLADE

The summer flew past, swift as a swallow. Then Jean Jacques Audubon was breathless at the sight of his first American autumn.

In France, autumn was a sad season of heavy mists and leaves lying wet on the ground. At Mill Grove it was a blaze of color. Blueberry bushes were like wildfire running over the hills. Sumac waved scarlet banners. Maple trees were bonfires against the blue sky.

The air smelled frosty when Jean Jacques picked up his long rifle and took his dog Zephyr out hunting. He was a strangely elegant young hunter in satin breeches and silk stockings. His hair curled to his shoulders. Silver mountings gleamed on the stock of his gun. He set out in high spirits.

"The lad is a gay young blade," Mrs. Thomas told her husband as they watched him off. "But there's no harm in him."

A couple of miles from Mill Grove, Zephyr stopped in his tracks. He whined, and the hair stood stiff along his back.

Jean Jacques grounded his rifle when he heard a hunter's boots crackling through dry leaves. He was much less happy about this meeting than the dogs were, for he was no longer on his own land. He did not like to be caught trespassing on another man's property. That it was the Englishman's land made it even worse.

The man who appeared was the very picture of an English hunter from scarlet coat to polished boots. Under his shooting cap, his weather-beaten face was ruddy. He held out his hand.

"You must be my neighbor, Mr. Audubon," he said with a friendly smile. "My name is Bakewell. William Bakewell."

They shook hands. Jean Jacques felt his hatred of Englishmen melting like hoarfrost in the sun. This man was a sportsman. Jean Jacques admired his manners and his hounds. He wanted to show off his own dog.

"Up, Zephyr!" he said. "Shake hands with the gentleman."

Zephyr walked on his hind legs across to Mr. Bakewell. He held up a paw and barked once.

Mr. Bakewell shook the paw. "I've heard about this fine dog from Friend Thomas. He has very pretty manners."

"Prettier than his master's, I fear," Jean Jacques apologized, "since I lacked the manners to return thy call."

"It's no matter; now we've met at last," Mr. Bakewell said kindly. "Young men are busy about their own affairs. I am admiring your gun, sir. I would not have expected a Quaker to own such a fowling piece, but I note that you say 'thee' and 'thou.' For that matter, I'd never met a Quaker in satin breeches."

53

Jean Jacques laughed, as Mr. Bakewell meant him to do. Then he did not feel embarrassed any longer. Before they parted, the roots of a strong friendship were well planted.

Jean Jacques called Mrs. Thomas as he burst into the house. "Are the ruffles on my best shirt starched? I'm going to call at Fatland Ford. It's a very remarkable man that lives there. Thou should see his dogs."

When the old lady smiled, Jean Jacques blushed. "I know what thou art thinking. Thou think I was one big fool before."

"Well, I see thou has come to thy senses—if this be thy senses." Mrs. Thomas gathered up the garments that Jean Jacques was pulling out and tossing aside for others. "Does thou pay this call *now*? I've been told the English make friends slowly."

"Oh, do they?" Jean Jacques was disappointed. "It is well thou told me. Now I shall not go to Fatland Ford until tomorrow."

When Jean Jacques dismounted at Fatland Ford the following day, he was starched to his last ruffle. He handed the reins of his sorrel horse to a servant boy. But the servant who answered his rap on the brass doorknocker said Mr. Bakewell was not in at the moment.

"Would you care to wait in the parlor, sir?"

Jean Jacques stepped into a large room where a bright fire burned. He did not see anybody there, only one of the hounds he had met yesterday.

"Good girl," he said to the hound.

Then a tall girl stood up from the inglenook where she had been sitting with her embroidery. Jean Jacques blushed.

"Oh, I did not mean—I—" He broke off and made her a very French bow.

"My father will be glad you came," said the girl. "I am Lucy Bakewell."

Lucy smiled sedately at the elegant young man. She hoped he would not guess that she was not yet quite sixteen years old. She picked up her embroidery hoop again. Jean Jacques sat and patted Juno the hound.

"Does thou like America?" he asked at last.

"I am not sure yet," Lucy said. "It is all so different from England. And you, Mr. Audubon, do you like America?"

"Better every day," Jean Jacques said quickly, smiling at Lucy. "But, pray do not call me Mr. Audubon. It sounds chilly." He shivered and made Lucy laugh. "My name is Jean Jacques," he went on. "Now that I live here, though, I try to say it always in English—John James. But I have another name I like better. It is LaForêt."

"LaForêt," Lucy repeated softly. "That means forest, doesn't it? I think that name suits you very well."

"I wish thou would call me LaForêt, Miss Bakewell."

Miss Bakewell, not quite sixteen, forgot her young lady airs. "I shall call you LaForêt if you call me Lucy."

They heard a quick giggle from the hallway. Lucy looked up. It was her little sister Eliza, of course, giggling. But she saw that all her brothers and sister were out there, peeking in at her visitor. She hoped young Mr. Audubon did not guess.

When Mr. Bakewell came into the house, the younger children vanished as if they had never been there.

That was the first of the many visits between Fatland Ford and Mill Grove. It was the beginning of a gay round of parties for the French boy. The whole countryside welcomed him now. As winter set in, there were balls and house parties.

"That Frenchman is the best dancer I've ever seen," Lucy's brother Tom said enviously. "But you had better watch out, sister, or you will lose him. All the ladies want him for a partner."

"Don't be so silly," Lucy said. But she blushed.

When the river froze, Tom saw that the Frenchman's skating was even more amazing than his dancing. He watched him skimming down the ice, with his long rifle over his shoulder. John James cut fancy figures and jumped across enormous airholes.

"Can you shoot, skating at full speed?" Tom called.

"Try me!" came the answer.

Up into the air flew Tom's new beaver hat. Down it came, riddled with buckshot at a distance of thirty yards. John James skated back to find Mr. Bakewell staring at the ruined hat.

"I should not have done that, sir," the boy apologized. "I am one big fool, always showing off."

"Then my son is one big fool, too," said Mr. Bakewell. "When he has to pay for a new best hat out of his allowance, he may learn a lesson."

Audubon was glad to escape to skate more sedately with Lucy. She was light as a bird on her feet, he thought. Pretty as a bird, too. John James Audubon knew no higher praise for beauty than that.

One morning all the young men skated miles up the Perkiomen to hunt ducks. It was past twilight before they thought of coming back. Skating was dangerous in the dark, with all the sharp bends and the airholes.

"You lead us back, John James," several boys said.

"Then follow my white flag, and no dawdling!" Audubon tied his big white handkerchief to a stick and held it high as he led the party swiftly down the frozen stream. With all their game, the boys were like a flock of ducks themselves, following their leader.

It grew darker. They skated faster and faster. There was no jumping airholes now. They had to circle them. Suddenly the leader vanished, white flag and all.

He had seen the airhole too late to stop himself—too late to swerve. The icy current caught Audubon and dragged him underneath the ice. His lungs felt as if they were bursting by the time he popped up through another hole forty yards farther downstream. Gulping in air, he tried to pull himself out of the river. His numbed fingers clutched at the snow, but it gave way. The stream was still sucking him down.

But at last he managed to crawl out onto thick ice.

He had no breath left to call his friends. When they found him, the young men shared their dry garments with him. This time the party got under way more carefully, and much more slowly.

When they reached the bank at Fatland Ford, Audubon felt as if he were burning and freezing at the same time. Mr. Bakewell met them. He had been anxious because they were so late.

"I play the big fool again, sir," Audubon managed to say through his chattering teeth. "I say that so often, now I begin to believe it." His laugh was shaky.

"Never mind, I'll put you right to bed here," Mr. Bakewell said. "I'll send word to the Thomases so they won't worry."

It was a week before Audubon went home. He found Lucy's attentions to an invalid very pleasant.

"Is there anything I can do for you, LaForêt?" she asked one day.

"Why, yes. Thou might teach me to speak the English better. Thou art my friend. It is from friends that we learn most of all."

By the time another spring blossomed along the Perkiomen, the English of John James Audubon was greatly improved. He gave up using the Quaker "thee" and "thou."

"Except I will always say them to thee, Lucy," he explained. "Then thou will know my words are meant only for thee."

Audubon found Lucy far less silly than any other girl he knew. She did not chatter and giggle when they walked in the woods. She watched birds in silence, as he did. She sat by the hour while he drew patient sketches.

"You will one day be a great artist, LaForêt," she said.

It was the right time to say those encouraging words. He had been disheartened because his birds still did not

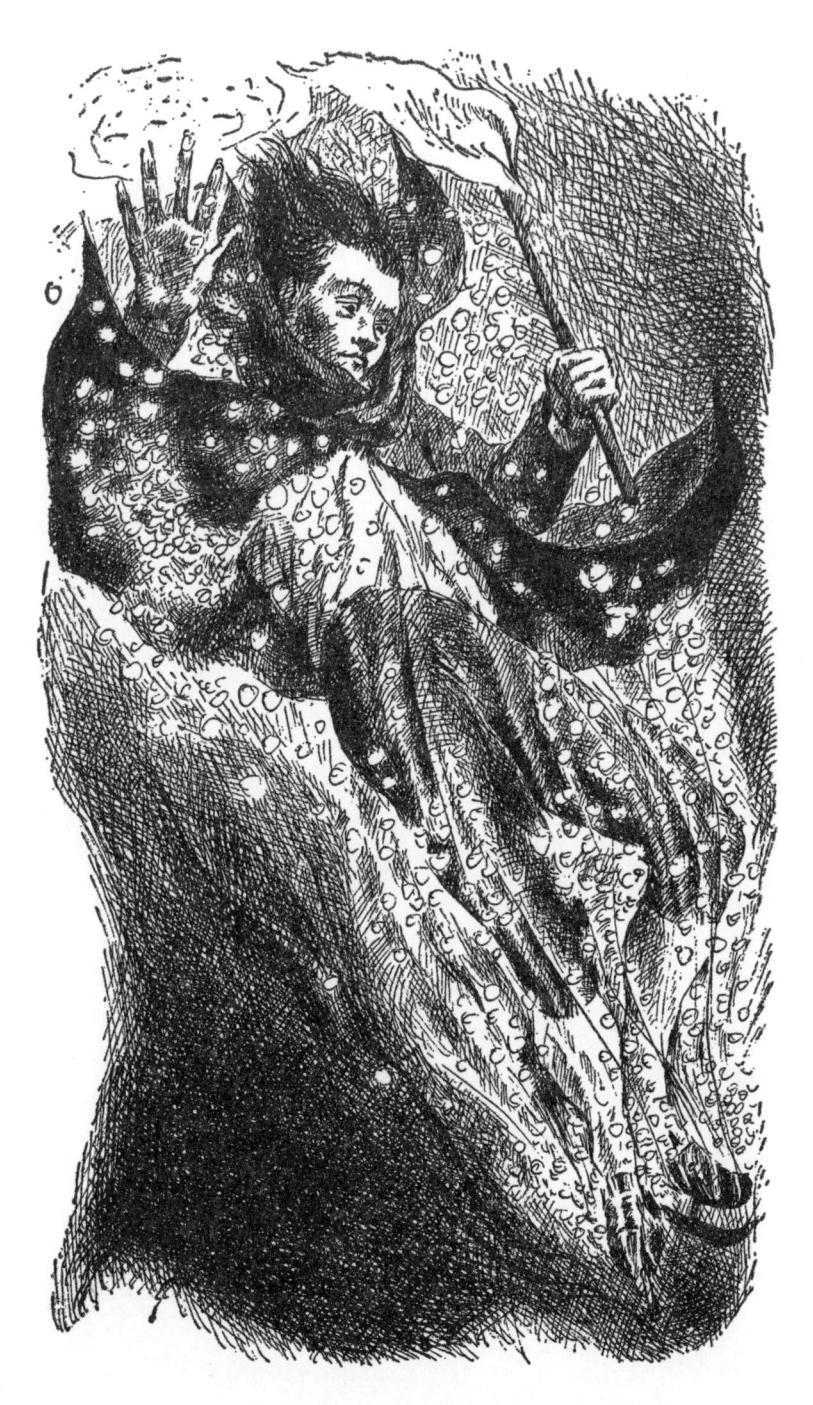

His lungs felt as if they were bursting

look as alive on paper as he wanted them to. But if Lucy believed he was going to be a great artist, then he believed it too.

Lucy was at the limestone cave with him the day the phoebes came back. They were wearing the silver thread bracelets on their legs.

All winter he had hoped they would come. But he had not been sure.

"I was right, Lucy," he whispered. "Does thou see I was right?"

"Yes, LaForêt." Lucy spoke softly, too, so she would not frighten the phoebes starting to spring clean their old nest. "I think you will always be right about birds."

CHAPTER EIGHT

JOHN JAMES MAKES A PROMISE

Lucy and Audubon wanted to get married. They thought this was a secret from everyone else in the world. They were both astonished when Mr. Bakewell guessed what they had come to tell him.

"Then you will give your consent, sir?" Audubon asked eagerly.

"Not so fast, young man." Mr. Bakewell held up his hand. "You know I like you as a friend. But I am not sure you would make my girl a good husband. How do you expect to earn the money to support a wife?"

"If it is only money, I have the answer for that," Audubon declared. "And it was a bird that gave me the answer."

Mr. Bakewell looked at him inquiringly.

"I was following a scarlet tanager," Audubon explained. "It flew into our old stone quarry. No one has used the quarry for years. But—I noticed lead ore showing in the rock. Friend Thomas and I had an expert come to look at it, and he says that vein of lead is a rich one."

In his excitement, Audubon was pacing around the sitting room.

"So now Mill Grove will have a lead mine," he went on. "We will make a nice fortune from it. Lucy and I will get married. It will make the fortune of my father, too. I have written, asking him to send a mining engineer to help us start the mine. When he comes, everything will be very fine."

But everything was far from fine when the man Captain Audubon had chosen as a mining engineer arrived at Mill Grove.

"I am your father's agent—Francis Dacosta," he introduced himself. "I have come to take charge here."

"To help us with the mine, you mean?" Audubon asked.

Dacosta smiled. "That will be my main interest since I am to be half owner of the mine," he said. "But your father has also told me to act as your guardian and tutor."

Audubon flushed, but he did not answer. He felt that since he was old enough to get married, he did not need a guardian or tutor. And he did not like Dacosta.

"But my father chose him to be his agent," he thought. "So we must try to work together."

This was difficult to do, however. Soon John James was sure that Dacosta was not trying to make money from the mine for the Audubon family. He was only trying to make it for himself. What was worse, he was also attempting to stir up trouble for John James and Lucy. Young Audubon learned about this when he received a letter from his father forbidding him to marry without permission.

"What have you been telling my father?" Audubon stormed at Dacosta.

"Only what is true—that he ought not to let you marry somebody whose family is not as good as yours," Dacosta replied calmly.

"I never heard such a lie in all my life!" Audubon said hotly. "The Bakewells are every bit as good as we are. I shall write my father all about it."

Dacosta's smile was sarcastic. "Which of us do you suppose the good Captain will believe, a boy without an ounce of sense in his head or the agent whom he trusts with his business?"

"He is wrong to trust you," Audubon cried. "I shall go to France and tell my father exactly what you are doing at Mill Grove. It is time he heard the whole story, and he will believe me once I see him."

Dacosta thought that might be true, and he did not want it to happen.

"Your father makes it clear he does not think it wise for you to be in France. Let me read you a sentence from the letter I have just had by the same post. 'The reasons which made me send the boy out there still remain.' By the way, what are those reasons, do you know?"

"If I did know, I wouldn't tell you," John James said furiously. "I still mean to go to France, and for that you must give me money."

"Not a penny!" Dacosta said. "Furthermore, the Captain has told me always to do as I see fit. So I am stopping your allowance until you come to your senses."

Audubon went on demanding money for his passage to France. At last Dacosta grew weary of the argument. He wrote a letter and handed it to the boy.

"Take this to Mr. Kauman at that address in New York. He is my banker, and he will give you the money for your fare."

"I need money to get to New York," Audubon pointed out.

"You won't get it from me. I have no cash at hand."

Audubon did not believe it. This was another attempt of Dacosta's to stop him. But it did not succeed. With only five shillings in his pocket, John James prepared to leave for New York.

He said goodbye to Lucy and Mr. Bakewell, only telling them that he had to go to France to see his father about the mining business. "And about my marriage, too," he added, with a glance at Mr. Bakewell.

"I think LaForêt ought to stay with Mrs. Palmer in New York, don't you, Papa?" Lucy said.

"Yes, that is a good idea. Mrs. Palmer," Mr. Bakewell told Audubon, "is a kinswoman and a very good friend to our family. And you must call on my brother Benjamin. He has an importing and exporting business. He might be useful to you since he knows the sailing schedules of all the ships."

Lucy walked to the door with Audubon. "Come back as soon as you can, LaForêt. The months will seem long without you."

"As soon as ever I can, I promise thee," said John James.

Then he set out on foot for New York. That winter was the coldest the country had known for fifty years. Snowdrifts made the roads all but impassable. But John James Audubon trudged along stubbornly, pulling himself out of one drift after another. He did not even have money enough to buy hot meals at the inns along the way. It was late at night on the third day when he arrived at Mrs. Palmer's address. He had walked more than one hundred and twenty miles through ice and snow.

Mrs. Palmer greeted him warmly. "Lucy's last letter was all about you," she told him with a smile. "I have always had great faith in Lucy's good judgment. Please consider this your home in New York."

Her kindness, together with a hot meal and comfortable bed, made Audubon's spirits soar. He felt extremely cheerful when he sought out Mr. Kauman the next morning.

Mr. Kauman looked no more pleasant nor trustworthy than Dacosta himself. Audubon explained why he had come. But when Kauman broke the seal on Dacosta's letter, he laughed out loud.

"You'll get no money from me," he said. "Dacosta wants me to have you arrested and shipped to Canton. He says you have given him a lot of trouble. So he is making arrangements with a sea captain to take you on a nice long voyage to China. I'll not help him with his dirty work, but I'll not give you any money either."

John James Audubon had never been so angry in his whole life. He was ready to walk straight back to Mill Grove. He had a very good sword there. And he was a good swordsman, too. He would make Dacosta pay dearly for his treachery.

Thankfully, he told both Mrs. Palmer and Benjamin Bakewell what he planned to do, and they were able to stop him. Lucy's uncle lent him money to pay for his passage on the first vessel sailing out of New York for France. Mr. Bakewell wanted to get the young man safely away before his anger against Dacosta could land him in real trouble.

The Audubon family at La Gerbetière had been excited about Rosa's coming marriage. But that was nothing to their excitement the day John James arrived there without a word of warning.

The Captain was at first speechless from astonishment. Madame cried over John James as she had often cried before. But this time she was crying for joy. And Rosa! She was no longer the little girl who hid under the bedclothes when an owl hooted. She was now a young lady with her dark hair piled high on her head.

"And here is my husband-to-be, LaForêt," Rosa said as a tall, uniformed man joined them in the hallway where they all still stood.

Audubon stared. It was Gabriel Loyen du Puigaudeau, the officer he had so disliked at the naval school.

"I'm not surprised that this comes as a jolt to you," Gabriel laughed as they shook hands.

Audubon suddenly realized that he no longer hated Gabriel at all. In fact, he seemed quite a nice fellow.

"Do you remember, Father, you told me I would change my ideas as I grew older?" John James asked when he followed the Captain into his study after dinner that evening. "You were right. I never expected to exchange a civil word with Gabriel. Now I find myself liking him. It's the same way with the English. I told you I would always hate them...."

"I remember," said the Captain, closing the door. "I am not so sure I am glad you changed your opinion there. Dacosta writes—"

"I can guess what Dacosta writes. That is why I am here—to tell you it is all a pack of lies."

"Dacosta says Lucy Bakewell is trying to marry you because her family thinks we are rich," Captain Audubon persisted.

John James laughed. "It is not that way at all, Father! The Bakewells have far more money and position than we have. Their house had not been built when you were in America, so you cannot know what Fatland Ford is like. Wait. Let me draw you a picture of it."

Captain Audubon knew the boy might exaggerate in his talk, but a picture was different. His drawings were always as accurate as he could make them.

The sketch of the mansion that grew before his eyes was very convincing: the big house with its imposing pillars, walled garden and handsome stables, and a picture of Mr. Bakewell standing before it, a man of substance and honesty.

"But if you are right, what reason can Dacosta have for making so much trouble?" the Captain asked.

A tall, uniformed man joined them in the hallway

"I've wondered a lot about that, Father," John James said. "I think he has been cheating you and that he was afraid Lucy's father might notice it where I would not."

It was an idea that had not occurred to the Captain.

"It is true that I have been pouring money into that mine," he admitted. "But still Dacosta claims he needs more expensive equipment."

"I doubt if all the money you have sent him has been spent on equipment," John James said.

"Well, I shall send him no more," the Captain told him. "I no longer have money to spend on that mine. In fact, here in France your *Maman* and I have only this place and my little pension from the Navy. I have even sold the house in Nantes."

"I wish you had told me this before," John James said. "I would have been more careful with my allowance."

"That was the smallest part of it. I felt a young man should have something to keep up his position.

"Now that you *are* a young man," the Captain went on, speaking very solemnly and lowering his voice, "I must talk with you about many things—things about your past that you have a right to know. When you were a child, it would have been dangerous to tell you. A child's careless word might have brought us great trouble in those days."

The Captain paused and glanced at the door of the study, to make sure it was closed. John James never took his eyes from the Captain's face. He knew that he was about to learn something important, something that might explain the many little broken pictures in the head of the child, Fougère—the little pictures that had never seemed to fit with anything else.

"You are old enough now so that I can talk to you with more freedom," the Captain continued. "But before I do, there is one promise I shall have to ask from you...."

Why the Captain made him promise, and what he told John James that evening at La Gerbetière, no one has ever discovered. All we know is that the promise which he made that night, John James kept as long as he lived.

CHAPTER NINE

THE NEW PARTNER

John James stayed in France longer than he expected. But it was not wasted time, for during these months he studied with Dr. d'Orbigny.

This young physician was a very good friend to Audubon. He was one of the greatest naturalists in France. He taught the boy all he knew about birds—how their bones were fitted together, why different kinds of birds had different kinds of beaks and feathers, and many other things. John James enjoyed studying with him.

Still, he was anxious to return to America and Lucy. Captain Audubon also had a reason for wanting his son to leave France now.

"This is not a good time for you to be here," the Captain told John James. "Napoleon is always looking for young men for his armies. This Napoleon! Crowning himself

Emperor, after all the trouble and fighting we had to make France a republic."

"Well, I am sure Lucy would not want me to be a soldier," John James said. "Did you get mail from America while you were in Nantes, Father?"

"I did. The brig *Polly* is in from New York, and my friend, Captain Sammis, handed me several letters. Mr. Benjamin Bakewell wrote, thanking me for repaying your passage money. He says he will be glad to help you in any way he can when you return. He even offered to give you a position as clerk in his exporting business."

"That is kind of him," John James said, without enthusiasm.

"The other Mr. Bakewell, his brother, also wrote."

"Lucy's father!" John James was eager now. "You can see how wrong Dacosta was about him, can't you, Father?"

"He sounds a most sensible and upright man," the Captain agreed. "I am now sure that you will never get on with Dacosta. What do you say to taking young Rozier out to Mill Grove as your partner? His father is anxious to send him to America, and he tells me the boy has a fine head for business. The two of you were friends as boys, weren't you?"

"Ferdinand Rozier?" John James asked. "He was all right, but a dreadfully dull fellow. He was never interested in anything but trading."

"You will have to think more about such things yourself now, if you mean to get married," said the Captain. "No more chasing birds in the woods."

John James sighed. Everybody was always at him to give up chasing birds, as if it were some kind of silly sport.

The Captain began fumbling in the leather mail pouch he had brought back with him from Nantes. His eyes

THE NEW PARTNER

twinkled when he finally pulled out the letter from Lucy that his son had been waiting for.

John James broke the seal. He became so engrossed, he barely heard his father say:

"I have had a talk with Captain Sammis. He intends to return soon to America. The *Polly* is laid up now while her keel is being scraped and her hull painted. But if you waste no time getting ready, you can sail on her."

"Oh, yes!" John James heard that all right. Then he went back to reading Lucy's letter again.

When the *Polly* was ready to weigh anchor, John James Audubon and his new partner, Ferdinand Rozier, were aboard her. After the ship had been at sea nearly three weeks, John James crossed her freshly scrubbed deck one morning to look over the rail.

"Ferdinand!" he called. "Come and look at these birds."

Rozier barely lifted his head. "I have something better to do than watch seagulls," he said. He chewed on a pencil.

"The gulls left us long ago," Audubon said. "These are the stormy petrels they call Mother Carey's chickens. I'd like to get close to them to see how they ride in the trough of the waves like that. I wish Captain Sammis would let me down in a dinghy."

"He would never be such a fool," Rozier said. He returned to his study of a long column of figures.

"What are you doing?" Audubon asked. "For days you've been at work with pencil and paper. It isn't even as if you were drawing anything. That looks like an arithmetic lesson."

"So it is, in a way." For the first time Rozier sounded enthusiastic. "I have been trying to find out how much money we can expect to make if we go into business."

Audubon shrugged his shoulders. He cared nothing about all these plans to make money. Talk about trade bored him. He kept watching the vast expanse of water and sky, looking for birds.

Rozier frowned. "Now that our fathers have made us sign partnership papers," he said severely, "I hope you are not the chucklehead you used to be. Do you know, anybody could cheat you when we were schoolboys in Nantes? One time I got you to give me a brand-new spinning top for one old egg—not even a whole egg, just a broken shell that had been hatched out. What a fool you were!"

"I remember that," Audubon said. "But I thought you were the fool. That was a shell I didn't have in my collection, and I would have paid a lot more than one top to get it."

"You would?" Rozier hated to think he had missed making the best possible trade even when he was a child. John James laughed out loud at the unhappiness on his partner's face.

Rozier went back to his figures rather sulkily. Audubon continued to lean on the rail. "There's another vessel coming up," he said a few minutes later. "She's fast, too."

Rozier looked then. He didn't see anything. He had never known anybody with such keen eyes and far sight as Audubon.

Audubon kept watching the other ship. When he saw Captain Sammis on the foredeck, he called to him. "Is that a pirate ship coming up, sir? I think she is chasing us."

The captain held his spyglass to his eye. "She does not fly a black flag," he said when he had inspected the other ship carefully.

Both the captain and Audubon went on watching. At last the other vessel maneuvered herself into position about half a mile off to starboard. Then she began to edge in closer.

Audubon saw a flash of flame and a puff of smoke. A cannonball had been fired right across the *Polly's* bow. A second and third shot brought every passenger onto the deck.

"Hide your valuables, everybody!" Captain Sammis ordered through a megaphone. "This is an English privateer. The English claim the right to search ships on the high seas for British seamen, so we shall probably be boarded. And some of the crew may be thieves."

There was a great scurry of people then. Rozier hung on tightly to the leather sack of money that had never left

75

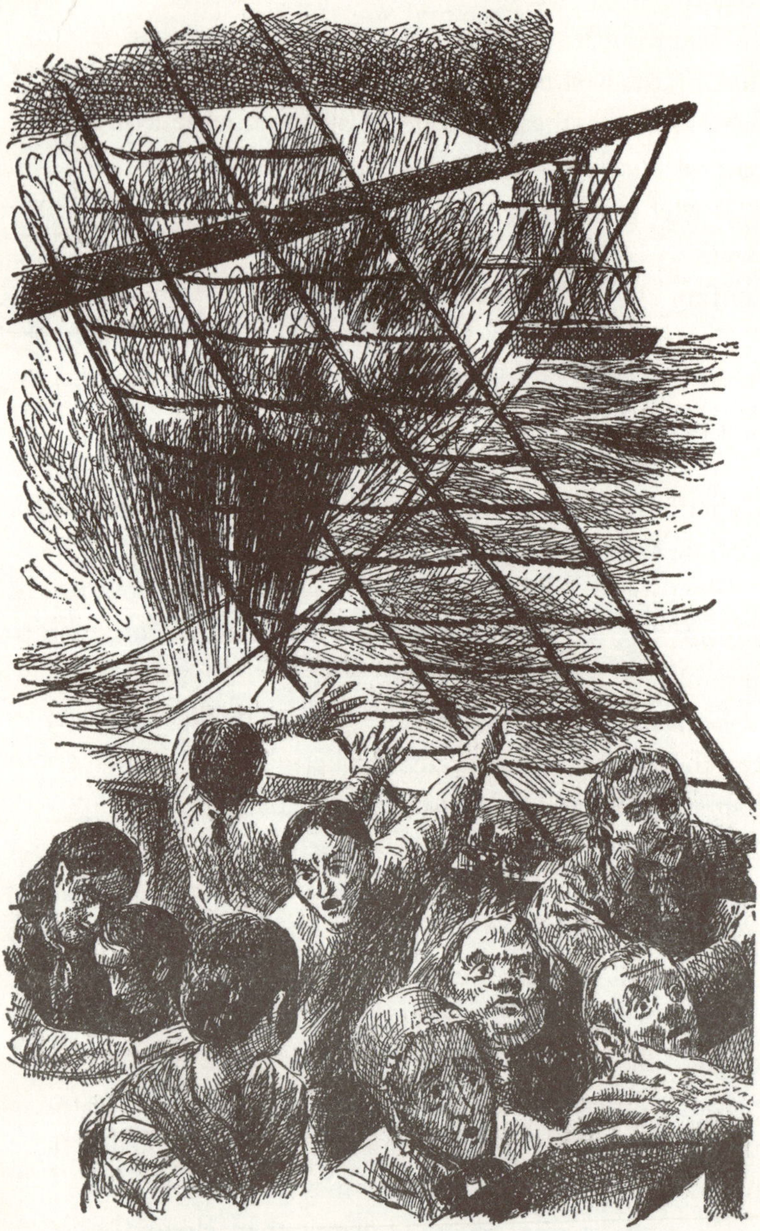

THE NEW PARTNER

him since they sailed. It was the gold which his father and Captain Audubon had given to him and John James to make their start in America.

"Is a privateer the same as a pirate ship?" he asked Audubon.

"Not exactly," Audubon laughed. "But sometimes their crews act as if they were."

By this time they could read the name *Rattlesnake* on the side of their pursuer. Audubon tried to snatch the money bag away from Rozier. "Give me that, and stop running about like a crazy hen."

"No!" Rozier said. "I will fight anybody who tried to take it!"

"Much good will it do you with a whole crew ready to board us!"

John James got hold of the sack and went forward into the bow. He stowed it away underneath a big coil of cable rope.

"We ought to be all right if they don't decide they need rope," he said. "Ferdinand, you stay away from here. Your face would give the whole show away."

An officer and boatload of sailors boarded the *Polly*.

"We are from the *Rattlesnake*," the officer told Captain Sammis. "Let me see your ship's clearance papers." He behaved as if he did not see the Stars and Stripes fluttering from the *Polly's* mainmast.

"Your papers seem to be pretty well in order," he admitted at last. "But we are going to keep you under our lee until we have searched you for runaway British seamen."

Captain Sammis protested, but for a whole day and night the *Rattlesnake* kept the *Polly* almost within pistol shot. The crew from the *Rattlesnake's* longboat boarded the *Polly* again and searched the ship from stem to stern. They made several trips back to their own vessel, taking pigs and sheep, and all the *Polly's* coffee and wines. They picked up some valuables, too, and two members of the *Polly's* crew. Their officer saluted Captain Sammis when he was about to drop overside into his gig for the last time.

"It's a very funny thing," Captain Sammis remarked bitterly, "how you fellows always manage to take our *best* seamen." He was very much relieved because all the valuables which had been hidden had not been discovered. But he did not want this man to guess that.

"Well," the officer laughed, "that may be because your

best seamen are British. They ought to be sailing with us to begin with."

When the *Rattlesnake* had finally left them, the commotion aboard the *Polly* was greater than ever. Passengers complained loudly that they had lost their purses. Ladies shrieked that their jewelry was gone. Ferdinand Rozier found Audubon standing on the coil of cable rope in the bow.

"Do you know," John James said, "there is not a single petrel left in these waters?"

"Never mind the birds! Where is our money?"

"It's safe enough where I stowed it," Audubon said.

Rozier could not believe it until he had the sack in his own hands again. "But I saw them up here talking to you, and I thought they searched you!"

"Oh, no," John James said airily. "I talk so much that they are glad to leave me alone."

"What did you talk about?"

"Birds. I stand on the rope, and I ask them all the questions about Mother Carey's chickens: when they come, why they come, where they go, and all that. I still want to know the answers, too, but they did not tell me."

"I can see why they left you alone," Rozier said.

Captain Sammis laughed when he heard about it. "This is a fine story to tell your father when next I see him," he told Audubon.

The voyage lasted eight weeks. To the boys it began to seem like years. Rozier was anxious to get ashore where the money would be safe. Audubon wanted to see Lucy and the birds at Mill Grove.

"By now, I have missed the return of my phoebes to their cave. But I will see them nesting. I wonder if any are wearing the silver bracelets."

Thirty miles off Sandy Hook, the wind freshened. The *Polly* began to roll and toss in the waves.

"You're as green as a fly-up-the-creek," Audubon told his partner. "Look at these gulls, will you? When they fly landwards, screaming like this, it's supposed to mean a bad storm coming."

"They're late," Rozier said. "We've already got the bad storm." He lurched over to the rail.

He soon learned that the storm was only beginning. The gulls were right. The wind continued to gather force until it was blowing a full gale. Then the passengers heard a scrunching noise. The *Polly* shuddered in all her timbers.

Captain Sammis groaned. "We're on a sandbar," he said. "These sands can suck a ship right down, too, till there's not a spar left of her. If we don't float off on this incoming tide, we'll have to abandon ship."

But at last his rough times were over. The flood tide lifted the *Polly* free to continue on her way to New York.

"Well, this is America," Audubon told Rozier at last. "How does it look to you, Ferdinand?"

Rozier looked at the ships in the busy harbor. He saw the people who crowded the wharf. People meant stores and trading to him. His spirits soared. "We ought to make our fortunes here," he declared happily.

CHAPTER TEN

MR. AND MRS. AUDUBON GO WEST

John James Audubon soon became a clerk in Mr. Benjamin Bakewell's importing business in New York. One day he was checking over a new shipment from France. At least, that is what he was supposed to be doing. But with all the gloves and laces and wines which had been sent from France, there had come a dozen music boxes. They all played the same tune. But each one was in a slightly different key.

Mr. Bakewell came into the office to see how his young clerk was getting on. He discovered him with every one of the little rosewood boxes tinkling away merrily.

"Do you hear, sir?" Audubon asked. "It is like birds' notes."

"No doubt," said Mr. Bakewell. "But playing music boxes will never hasten your marriage to my niece. And I am told that you waste many hours along the waterfront, watching seabirds."

Young Mr. Audubon felt a stirring in his pocket. He put his hand in to quiet the tiny creature that was waking up there. Somehow, he did not think that Mr. Bakewell would approve of his bringing a pet screech owl to work. He sighed. His marriage to Lucy seemed farther away than ever.

It was almost two years since he and Ferdinand Rozier had arrived from France. They had soon found they could never work with Dacosta. So they sold him their share of the farm and mine. Then they set out to gain experience in business. Rozier went to work in Philadelphia in a place where he could learn English. And Audubon was here.

He spent his days in Mr. Bakewell's counting house. In the evening he stuffed and mounted bird and animal specimens for the museum of his new friend, Dr. Samuel Mitchell. He learned a lot from Dr. Mitchell, who was a famous naturalist, and he enjoyed the work, for it gave him a chance to study bones and plumage and fur.

His boardinghouse neighbors did not enjoy it a bit, however. They complained as Rosa used to do about the smells which came from his room. One morning when he set out for work, a man was waiting for him at the door.

"Mr. Audubon? I am a constable. Your fellow lodgers have reported to me that you are a public nuisance."

"Nuisance?" Audubon asked, raising his eyebrows. "Me? I bother nobody. I make no noise."

"It is the smells they object to," said the constable. "You will have to move."

Audubon wondered where he could live. "This city is no place for a man of the outdoors," he told himself as he climbed the steps to the counting house. "I'll never be happy in the city or in the counting house, either."

The question of being happy in the counting house was already settled for him, he discovered. He found Mr. Bakewell looking upset.

"I hate to tell you this, my boy," he said, "but you do not belong here."

"I suppose not, sir," Audubon admitted. "Have I done something especially bad?"

"It was certainly not good," Mr. Bakewell said. "Yesterday you sent eight thousand dollars out of this counting house through the mail. You did not even seal the envelope it was in."

After this, Mr. Bakewell did not want Audubon in his business. But he was still willing to help him for Lucy's sake. When Audubon and Rozier decided to open a store of their own in Louisville, Kentucky, Mr. Bakewell helped them get together a stock of goods.

Louisville, on the Ohio River, was only a frontier town in those days. It was not an easy place to reach. The goods for the new store had to be sent westward from Philadelphia in covered wagons. The partners went by stagecoach through the mountains to Pittsburgh. There they waited three weeks for the wagons to catch up with them. Then they loaded their merchandise on a flatboat and floated down the beautiful Ohio River till they came to Louisville. As soon as they got the store started, Audubon hurried back to Fatland Ford to claim Lucy as his bride.

"I'm glad you're here in time to greet the phoebes, LaForêt," Lucy said. They were sitting in the pale spring sunshine at the mouth of the cave, soon after his arrival. "It has been such a warm spring. I was afraid they would get here ahead of you. Now tell me all about Louisville."

"Ah, Louisville. Dost thou know, there are buffalo and deer roaming the Silver Hills that circle halfway around that town?" John James asked her enthusiastically. "The river is so full of fish by the rapids that thou can see them jumping. And birds, I can't begin to tell thee about them! Why, I saw one flight of passenger pigeons darken the air for two whole days as they passed overhead. Everybody was shooting them."

Audubon did not like the idea of killing without reason. But even he could not guess that a hundred years later, there would not be a single passenger pigeon left anywhere in the United States.

"And you and Ferdinand Rozier have a store?" Lucy asked practically.

"Oh, a fine store in a log house," replied Audubon. "There are already a thousand people in Louisville, and more arrive almost every day, not counting Indians. We ought to do very well."

"Are there many French people there, LaForêt?"

"A number," said Audubon. "There are even some of our old aristocrats who fled from France during the Revolution. One of them is my especially good friend. She calls herself now Madame Berthoud, but once her husband was a noble in the French court, and she was lady-in-waiting to Queen Marie Antoinette herself. Madame Berthoud will welcome thee for my sake. But she will love thee for thy own sake."

Lucy looked at LaForêt. She saw him as that old French aristocrat must see him, very handsome and with all the elegance of an aristocrat himself. She decided he must be one of that old nobility.

"LaForêt, you told me once there have been many changes of name in your own life. Is there some secret about that?"

Audubon looked troubled. "There is, Lucy, but I cannot tell it even to thee. At least, not yet. I gave my solemn promise not to reveal my true name. But the name of Audubon I revere, for I have cause to be grateful to it."

"Then I, too, shall be proud to have the name of Audubon," Lucy said. "And as for your secret, I shall just forget about it. I would not have you break a promise. I think, though, that we had better not tell anyone else that there *is* a secret, not even Papa. He might not understand, and we do not want anything to stand in the way of our wedding."

"Nothing must ever come between thee and me again, Lucy. We shall start west, just thee and I and Zephyr, and such sights as I shall show thee! Such birds! How long must we wait to be married?"

"Five days," Lucy told him with a smile.

Five days later, the Reverend Dr. Latimer, a minister from Philadelphia, arrived at Fatland Ford in his carriage. A purple ribbon marked the marriage service in his prayer book. The windows of the big house blazed across the whole countryside with the lights from the wedding candelabra.

Mr. and Mrs. Thomas came over from Mill Grove, but Mr. Dacosta was not invited. Servants bustled about seeing that house guests from Philadelphia and New York, and even from Boston, were made comfortable with fires in their bedrooms and silver warming pans between their sheets. Lucy's little sister Eliza cried herself into hiccups because she could not go west, too.

As soon as the wedding was over, Mr. and Mrs. Audubon set out in a coach over a rough road which led westward to Pittsburgh. Lucy had never been in such wild country before, but she looked at everything through her husband's eyes. She was so happy she sang a little song as the coach bowled along through the mountains.

Suddenly, at a dangerous pass, a wheel rolled off down the hill. The coach turned over and slid, dislodging a small avalanche of rocks. Lucy was painfully bruised and shaken.

"I should never have brought thee away from thy home," Audubon cried as he gathered her up in his arms. "Thou might have been killed!"

"But I was not killed, and you could not have left me behind, LaForêt. I wouldn't let you. If I am to be the wild bird's mate, then I shall build my nest in the wilderness, and it will be home."

A wheel rolled off down the hill

CHAPTER ELEVEN

A NEW WORLD FOR LUCY

On her wedding journey from Pittsburgh to Louisville, Lucy Audubon saw the Ohio River as a world of wings, of clear water and islands and forested banks. With each hundred miles they traveled, the farms grew scarcer. At last even the blue smoke from a lone squatter's cabin was a rare sight.

"Fewer people, but more birds," Audubon said happily. He pointed out a flight of wild geese winging their way northward.

"It is a good thing I am not jealous, LaForêt," Lucy said with a smile. "Every bird is my rival."

"Thou knows that is not so. There is no other like thee."

Lucy laughed. "Well, I should hate to put it to a test."

The flatboat in which they were floating was called an ark. Sometimes it seemed as if it held as many animals as Noah's Ark. There were cows, sheep, pigs, dogs, cats, and chickens. All the other young couples aboard were seeking frontier homes. Some of them had small children. All of them had brought their possessions along. The deck was piled high with featherbeds, spinning wheels, and stoves.

When the travelers needed meat, the ark was tied up to a tree by the bank. The men took their guns. In a few minutes, they would bring back enough teal and grouse and turkey for a feast. The smell of roasting fowl mingled with scents of sweet fern and moss.

As twilight closed in, nighthawks swooped along the shore. With real darkness, the whippoorwill call sounded in the mysterious depths of the forest. Then John James brought out his fiddle and played old tunes from France and new tunes he had learned in America.

Everyone but Audubon was usually asleep in the morning when the earliest songs began. But he never missed them: cheerful chirpings of robins, the rattle of kingfishers and flickers, the three-noted song of the wood thrush, and then a huge chorus from thrashers and singing sparrows, tanagers, and orioles. The woodpecker accompanied these songs with his drumming.

Louisville, when at last they reached it, was interesting to Lucy. It was a thriving little town with a strange mixture of people. Silent Indians mingled in the muddy streets with buckskin-clad scouts and traders and finely dressed French aristocrats.

As Audubon had promised, Madame Berthoud welcomed Lucy. They had long talks together. Sometimes the distinguished old lady in her silks and laces told Lucy stories of her life at the court of the King and Queen of France. Perhaps Madame Berthoud was also able to tell Lucy part, at least, of Audubon's secret. If she did, Lucy did not talk about it to anyone else.

Rozier had also welcomed them, glad that Audubon could now help him in the store. He had made arrangements for the young Audubons to live at the Indian Queen Tavern. This inn was built around an open courtyard, where all the guests were obliged to gather at the pump to wash. The mattresses were of husks, and it was so crowded that most of the rooms housed six and eight people. Audubon and Lucy were happy to have a room to themselves as their first home. It was at the Indian Queen that their first baby was born. They called him Victor.

"That is a name to live up to!" Audubon said, tickling his tiny son until he opened his mouth in a toothless smile. "And someday soon we shall have a real home of our own for him."

Audubon meant to work hard in the store, as Rozier did. But the country was so full of wild birds and animals that temptation proved too much for him. He began drifting away from the counter. Rozier grumbled that he was left to do all the work.

"But, you see, LaForêt must have time, too, for his real work," Lucy said. "There are things more important than making a living. My husband is a great artist."

"You shouldn't encourage him," Rozier warned her.

Lucy was beginning to dislike Rozier. He did nothing but complain, she felt. Part of his bad temper was due to the fact that business was not as good as he had expected it to be. That was not Audubon's fault. But Rozier blamed him for it anyway.

Audubon quickly made friends with the Osage and Shawnee Indians. They taught him their language. They showed him how to make soup of nuts and bear fat, and which herbs were good for medicine. In moccasins like theirs, Audubon soon could walk over twigs and dry leaves without making a sound. By the time he met Daniel Boone near Frankfort, he was almost as good as that old scout at blazing a trail through trackless forest. On every trip he took along paper and crayons.

Lucy used to smile at him in his torn deerskin jacket, his scuffed moccasins, and leggings. He wore a tomahawk fastened to his belt. It was a present from an Osage chief.

"My, to think I remember when you hunted in silk stockings and knee breeches and the ruffliest shirts this side of the Atlantic Ocean," she teased him.

"Don't remind me of it, dear Lucy!" Audubon protested. "I must have looked funny enough to make a bird laugh."

Audubon quickly made friends with the Indians

On one of the mornings when Audubon was working in the store, he met a stranger who surprised him. A shabby little man came in who looked both ill and unhappy. But Audubon had eyes mostly for the little green parakeet perched on his shoulder.

"I am Alexander Wilson," the odd-looking stranger introduced himself. "I am selling books. Bird books. They are not all published yet, but I can show you some. I have to take subscriptions now so I can pay my printer, but when my books are completed they will contain the only drawings of birds in America."

"But I too draw birds!" Audubon pulled his portfolio from beneath a bolt of calico where he had hidden it. There was real astonishment on Wilson's face when he saw the drawings.

"I had no idea," he said slowly, "that anyone else was engaged in this work. Do you intend to publish these?"

"I had not known it was possible to publish such pictures," Audubon said truthfully. "I paint birds for my own pleasure."

Audubon could not afford to subscribe to Mr. Wilson's *American Ornithology*. He was able to show him some new specimens of birds before he left Louisville, but the two men never became friends.

"I wish I had been able to help him," Audubon told Lucy. "He knows a great deal about birds."

"Not as much as you do," Lucy said. "And if men can publish bird paintings, then one day you must have yours in a book for all the world to admire."

Meanwhile business in the store had been poor, and Rozier was sure that they could not be successful in Louisville. "A fresh start is what we need," he told Audubon.

"That, and to have you turn over a new leaf and really get to work."

"Where do you propose we make this fresh start?" Audubon asked. "Afterward, we can see about my new leaf."

"I hear that Henderson, farther down the Ohio, is a thriving new town," said Rozier. "Let us move our business there."

Audubon was willing. So they loaded a flatboat with all their goods. Then Rozier and the little Audubon family set out downriver. Victor was one year old and just beginning to notice the creatures that fly. Audubon spent most of the trip pointing out birds to his small son. Rozier spent his time wondering how much money they could make in Henderson.

Henderson claimed to be thriving, but the newcomers found it only a huddle of log houses surrounded by land covered with giant cane. Less than two hundred people lived there. Rozier soon discovered that most of them were poor.

The Audubons liked the place. They found good friends in Dr. Rankin and his wife. Dr. Rankin had been a well-known physician in the East, but he had come to Henderson because he, too, loved the wilderness. He helped Audubon build their log cabin home. The finest piece of furniture in it was the cradle John James made for his son Victor. Lucy found it, as well as her cabin home, entirely delightful. She did not sigh for the elegance of Fatland Ford. She was truly the mate of the wild bird now. The wilderness was all home to her.

Audubon did not turn over any new leaf. Canebrake and woods were too full of new birds. He spent less and less time in the store. Rozier did more and more grumbling. He came to complain to Lucy, but Lucy would hear no word against her husband.

Rozier stood one day with his back to the log fire. His hands were clenched in his pockets. "You defend him, Madame," he said. "You always do that. Why do you not look at facts? Your husband is simply off bird's-nesting like a boy. He cannot make money that way."

Lucy bent over the cradle to tuck in Victor's blanket. Then she turned to Rozier.

"I do face facts, Mr. Rozier. They just happen not to be your facts. My husband is not meant for business. I wouldn't blame you for breaking the partnership. I wish you would, for together you two will never do each other any good."

"You do not like me, Madame Audubon," Rozier said. "But I admire you. Only you have no common sense. I have seen what you were used to at Fatland Ford. Look at this room! Make your husband do right!"

Lucy looked at the room. She saw a place she loved. She smiled at Rozier. "You will never understand. Great artists are always hard to understand."

CHAPTER TWELVE

THE PARTNERSHIP ENDS

"I know, I know!" Rozier thumped the splintery wooden counter until a bolt of red calico bounced on it. "Your wife wants us to break our partnership. But an agreement ought to be binding."

"Am I a man to break his word?" Audubon said with dangerous calm. "I only asked what you thought of the idea. It is, after all, you who do all the complaining."

"Now, Jean Jacques, do not be angry." Rozier knew from their boyhood that it was not wise to rouse Audubon's temper. "It is this wretched town of Henderson that is causing our trouble. No one could make a penny here. But I have heard of a new place, Sainte Geneviève. Everyone is French there, and that will help us.

"It is on the great Mississippi River where there is much more trade. If Madame Audubon and Victor could stay with your friend Dr. Rankin for a few weeks, we might go and see if there is an opportunity there for us."

"On the Mississippi, eh? Let us go then." Just in time Audubon stopped himself from saying he had been wanting to see what birds lived along the Mississippi.

It had been snowing all night. It was still snowing on the December morning when they set out by boat for Ste. Geneviève. Snowflakes caught in Lucy's dark curls as she stood on the bank to see Audubon off. She held up Victor's little mittened hand to wave goodbye to his father.

Audubon thought this new boat very fine. It was a keelboat, with shining brass trimmings. There was a cabin in the bow. The boat was sent downriver by men who rowed with four sturdy oars and a steersman with a sixty-foot steering oar in the rear. Along with his master, Zephyr inspected the craft from bow to stern.

"Why did you bring that old hound?" Rozier asked. "He's no use."

"He is old," Audubon admitted. "But old friends are best, eh, Zephyr? You shall never be left behind while you want to come with me."

Zephyr wagged his tail. Rozier went into the cabin to get warm.

It snowed for a week, by day and by night. The wind whipped the calm Ohio River into white-capped waves. Audubon was first to notice the chunks of ice floating along beside the boat.

"I hope we get to St. Louis before the Mississippi is filled with ice," the captain said. He had begun to look worried.

At Cash Creek, just before reaching the great river, they learned that the Mississippi was already ice jammed. They could not go on. Looking behind them at the Ohio, they saw there was no going back either.

"Well, folks," the captain told his fifteen passengers, "I reckon you're here till the spring thaw."

They landed, and everybody pitched in to make camp. They put up windbreaks and lean-tos of thick boughs. They made beds out of branches. Buffalo robes and cooking pots were carried from the boat.

As he built a fireplace, Audubon sang. Here he was, hemmed in by vast untouched forest. He had all the time and freedom of a long winter to follow birds and animals. He had drawing supplies. What more could a man want?

Rozier wanted a great deal more. He wanted a warm house and a store. He wanted customers. Here, he stayed rolled up in his buffalo robe when he was not trying to figure out how much money he might make in Ste. Geneviève. Soon, he slept most of the day.

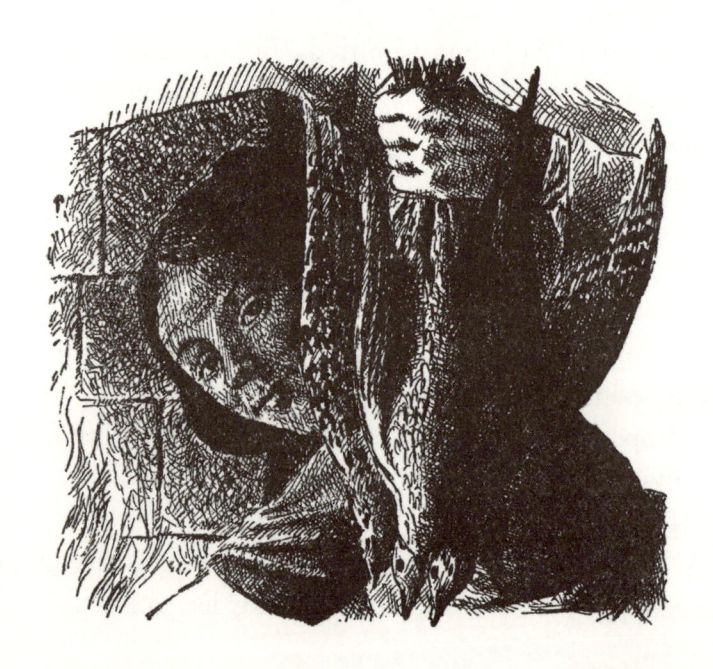

"You look like a squirrel in winter quarters," Audubon laughed, when only the tip of Rozier's nose poked out of his buffalo robe.

On Christmas morning, even Audubon was homesick for Lucy and Victor. Then he remembered something interesting. At the edge of a lake yesterday, he had noticed an Indian camp. He whistled for Zephyr, and the two of them set out to get acquainted over there.

The friendly Osages welcomed this white visitor. He was eating a fish breakfast that the squaws cooked for him when he heard strange calls on the lake. He looked out to see hundreds of whistler swans. Their white plumage was dazzling in the sun. In shadow it looked almost bluish. The swans were dipping their long bills into the lake water. They were having a fish breakfast, too.

It made a picture too lovely to lose. Audubon pulled out sketchbook and crayons. The Indians were fascinated by his quick drawing.

"The Bird People are your people," one of them said to him.

The Osages took Audubon hunting with them through dark, deep forest. The only sound was the hacking of tomahawks on trees where a new trail was being blazed.

They reached a clear glade, and one of the men began to dance. It looked like a war dance. Around and around he circled, pointing to the sky. Looking up, Audubon saw a huge brownish-black bird flying so low he could make out its feathers and coloring.

"What is it?" he asked.

"Big Chief," the Indian man told him. "Big Chief Bird."

Audubon could readily believe it was a Big Chief among the birds. For some reason it reminded him of the Big

Chief whose portrait had hung at Mill Grove, the Big Chief General Washington.

"I am going to call it the Bird of Washington!" he declared. He did that, too. It was the American bald eagle.

He stayed for dinner with the Indians. It was a good meal of pecan nut soup and venison. Afterwards, they all wanted to watch him draw. They laughed when he did a portrait in red chalk of the chief's sister.

Now that they were his good friends, Audubon often visited the Osages. He and Zephyr thoroughly enjoyed their winter. The rest of the party did not. They grew very tired of the food. It was mostly turkey meat, so dry they served it buttered with bear fat.

Then came the spring thaw. The captain's black eyes blazed with excitement.

"The ice is melting, and we're on our way!"

Rozier came to life and rolled out of his blanket. Only Audubon thought it was too bad that they must leave.

However, the broad waters of the Mississippi were new to John James. So he was soon eager to study new birds and animals along these shores. But when they reached Ste. Geneviève, the little French settlement below St. Louis, he did not like it at all.

"It is dirty," he said. "These Frenchmen are ignorant and bad-tempered. I would not bring my wife and child here."

"But we can make a fortune here," Rozier protested. "And we do not need to wonder what goods to buy for our store. Gunpowder! And you can sell all you offer."

"Ferdinand, you are impossible!" exclaimed Audubon. "Money, money, money. That is all you think about."

"You, too, are impossible!" Rozier replied hotly. "Birds, birds, birds. That is all *you* think about. Your wife says you

One of the men began to dance

are a great artist. But I say I do not need a great artist to help me sell gunpowder. I like you in a way, Jean Jacques. But now I agree that we must break up our partnership."

So at last the two partners said goodbye, each glad to be rid of the other. But Audubon was the happier of the two. He would now have a long, long walk back to Henderson, but it would be through the wild forest that he loved. Before starting out, he made sure that he had plenty of drawing paper and crayons with him.

CHAPTER THIRTEEN

A HORSE NAMED BARRO

As he tramped through lonely stretches of forest on his way home to Lucy, John James Audubon whistled. Birds answered him. Zephyr padded along at his heels. At night they lay side by side on the ground, and Audubon listened to the night birds.

At twilight one evening he chanced upon a lone cabin. A tall, untidy woman stood near the door. She stared silently at him until he pulled out his watch to see the time.

"You sleep here!" she said then. "There's a cake in the ashes on the hearth and plenty of cooked venison. Can I look at that? How much is it worth?"

"It is a good watch," Audubon said as he handed it to her. "I brought it from France." He accepted her invitation without surprise. Frontier people usually expected travelers to be their guests.

Inside the cabin, Audubon found an Indian boy sitting dejectedly in front of the fire with his head in his hands. He was in great pain, for little more than an hour before, one of his arrows had split and blinded one of his eyes. Audubon tried to talk to him, but the boy did not understand the only Indian language that Audubon knew. When the woman was not looking, however, he got up, walked past Audubon, and pinched him hard on the arm.

While Audubon shared a thick slab of venison with Zephyr, the boy drew out his knife and tomahawk. Audubon felt chilled by the glare from the Indian's one bright eye.

There were no beds in the cabin, but a pile of bearskins lay in the corner.

"You can have one," the woman told Audubon.

"Thank you, Madame," he said. "Now may I have my watch again? I want to wind it."

The woman had put the watch on its gold chain around her dirty neck. She was still wearing it, but she gave it up reluctantly. Audubon lay down on a bearskin, with Zephyr stretched out beside him. He pretended to sleep, but he kept his hand on his gun.

An hour later, the woman's strong young sons came in with guns over their shoulders. They wanted to know what the Indian and Audubon were doing there.

"Hush!" the woman said. She began whispering while they all gathered around her. Audubon caught the word "watch." He felt Zephyr quiver and put his hand on the old hound to keep him quiet. The woman picked up a carving knife and left the cabin. Then from outdoors, Audubon caught the whine of the knife being sharpened on a grindstone.

The woman came back and handed the knife to one of her sons. "There, settle him!" she whispered, motioning to the Indian. Taking a gun which one of her boys had left by the chimney place, she crept toward Audubon.

As Audubon jumped up, the door was flung open. Two stout travelers stood there with their guns leveled. The Indian boy came to life. He helped the others tie up the woman and her sons and dump them against the wall. Then he capered in a dance. He talked to the newcomers, who understood his language.

"He says he kept doing his best to warn you," one of the men told Audubon, "but there was never a minute when either of you could escape. It was good we had been told about these villains. And it was better still that we chose tonight to investigate their doings. You are not the first man they have attacked and robbed. But you take chances traveling alone this way. It is not safe."

Audubon laughed. "I've done a great deal of it," he said. "And this is the only time I've ever been in danger from my fellow man. I am very glad you came when you did and glad to leave these three in your hands, too. My dog and I will finish our night's slumber in the woods."

The next morning, Audubon, with Zephyr, started off again. The soft spring air filled with sweet bird songs soon raised his spirits. He did not tell Lucy about his narrow escape when he got home, so as not to worry her.

A short time later, a stranger arrived from the headwaters of the Arkansas. He wanted to sell his horse.

"He's no beauty, is he?" Audubon remarked.

"No," the owner admitted, "but he's clever. He's a wild plains horse that I caught and broke myself."

"What is his name?" Audubon asked.

"Barro. You can try him, if you like. His gaits are good for comfortable riding, and he's not gun shy, you will find."

Barro's mane was long and thick and full of burrs. His tail was thin and droopy. But his chest was deep, and his legs were strong. Though he had never worn shoes, his black hoofs were not split.

Audubon tested Barro in the woods, jumping logs lightly as a circus pony. In swamps the horse was cautious, keeping his nose near the water as if to judge the depth. From the saddle, Audubon shot a wild turkey. Barro went up to the bird like a bird dog.

"You've made a sale!" Audubon said. "What does he especially like to eat when I want to give him a treat?"

The man laughed. "He has a rare fancy for hens' eggs and pumpkins."

One day Audubon was jogging along on Barro when he saw the western sky turn black. He heard a rumbling like a violent tornado.

"Pick up your feet, Barro," he said. "Let's get to some house before this thunderstorm breaks."

For the first time, Barro refused to obey. He scarcely moved, setting one foot stiffly before the other as if he walked on eggs. Audubon thought he had gone lame. As he was about to dismount, Barro neighed shrilly. Then he stood still as if bracing himself against some mighty force.

Barro's master saw the earth begin to move. Cracks appeared along the ground. The earth shuddered, heaved, and waved until Audubon felt seasick. Barro just stood, still braced.

As suddenly as it had darkened, the sky grew light. The earthquake was over. Barro raised his head and set out briskly along the trail home. Audubon rushed into the house to make sure that Lucy and Victor were safe.

"What I don't understand," he told Lucy, "is how Barro knew it was coming. And he knew what to do about it."

"Well," Lucy said, "Barro took good care of you, LaForêt. For that he shall have two eggs *and* a pumpkin for his supper tonight."

That was the beginning of a series of earthquakes throughout the West. Islands sank out of sight. Old lakes disappeared, and new ones formed in other places.

Once when Audubon and Barro were drinking together at a stream, Audubon lifted his head to see a great yellow spot in thick haze. In another instant the forest was in turmoil, creaking, bending, whirling. Branches and leaves and dust were swept along in a gigantic hurricane. The sky was a queer greenish color. The air smelled strangely.

"So now we have gone through a hurricane together, Barro," Audubon said when it was over. He was leading his horse in a scramble over great uprooted trees. "I reckon nothing would upset you."

Before the year was over, a comet trailed its fiery tail across the sky. "It's the end of the world!" people began saying.

One night, a shrill shrieking brought the people of Louisville tumbling out of their beds. They ran outdoors, not knowing what to expect now. This time it was not one of nature's surprises. It was the new steamboat *Orleans*, the first ever to come up the Ohio River.

When the monster reached Henderson, people there had already heard about it, so they were not so frightened as the Louisville people had been. The whole town gathered on the wharf to watch for it.

Audubon hurried Barro along, so he would be in time. "Come now," he pressed his knees against Barro's sides, "one short gallop and we're there."

The steamboat had been chugging along at five miles an hour. Suddenly it let off steam with a scream like the end of the world.

Barro stopped so short in his tracks that his rider shot right over his head. The horse had been calm during earthquake and hurricane. He had not even looked at the comet. But this manmade monster was too much for his nerves.

Audubon laughed as he picked himself up. He was still laughing when he got to the wharf. The *Orleans* was not making a stop at little Henderson. But as she steamed close, John James dived into the river and swam underneath the boat to come up on the other side.

"You are a madman!" everybody was saying when he climbed out of the water. "It might have exploded on top of you! Who knows how dangerous machines like that can be?"

"I only wanted to see what the underside of a steamboat was like," Audubon told Lucy, who stood on the dock holding Victor.

"You will never grow up, LaForêt!" Lucy scolded him.

Little Victor laughed. "Papa do it again?" he asked hopefully.

CHAPTER FOURTEEN

A CLOUD WITH A SILVER LINING

Victor was playing with his little brother John by the duck pond. He thought they were the blessed boys in the world. Nobody else had such interesting pets as Papa was always bringing home to them. There was a lame trumpeter swan and a sparrow hawk called Nero, who perched on Barro's back while he grazed. There was a wild turkey, too, which had been a helpless fledgling when they named him Orphan. Now he acted like a cock of the barnyard, bossing the geese and hens.

The two boys stopped their game when they saw a strange man come into their yard. "Where's your pa, young'uns?" he asked them. "I want to talk with him."

"You can't," Victor answered. "Papa's most terribly busy learning to draw with his left hand. His right hand got hurt at the mill."

Both boys let out a whoop when the man kept on toward the house. "Minnie! There's a man wants to bother Papa."

Ever since they were babies, they had called their mother Minnie. It was the Scotch word for mother, and Lucy liked it.

"Good morning, Sheriff!" Lucy said quietly in the doorway. "My husband really is very busy. Won't I do?"

The sheriff looked uncomfortable. "No, ma'am, I'm afraid not. I have come to arrest him because of all his debts."

The sheriff's visit did not surprise Lucy. Soon after Audubon had returned to Henderson, he had built her this lovely house, where little John had been born. Then he and her brother Tom had gone into business together. They had built a big mill.

But they had never made money with the mill. It could grind wheat, but the people in Henderson did not grow wheat. It could saw logs, but expert axemen would not pay to have logs sawed. Tom had given up at last and gone back East, but Audubon kept on trying. He used the mill to saw planks, and with them he hired some men to help him build a steamboat. When it was finished, he sold it to a man who paid him with a bank check which was worthless. By the time Audubon discovered this, the man and the steamboat were far down the Mississippi River.

In a skiff, Audubon chased that scoundrel all the way to New Orleans. But he was too late. The steamboat had already been taken over by other people to whom the man owed money. When he got back home, months later, Audubon had only an ivory-billed woodpecker and two new bats to show for his trip. And the mill still held one more trouble in store for him. It had crushed his right hand. And now the sheriff was here to arrest him.

"Perhaps we can pay the debts," Lucy said. "There are my husband's drawings. They are very valuable."

"That's no good," the sheriff told her. "They may be valuable to you, ma'am, but nobody will pay money for pictures of birds."

The sheriff took Audubon away to the jail in Louisville. Then everything the family owned had to be sold to pay the debts: the mill and Audubon's wonderful horse Barro, the house and all the furniture, Lucy's silver tea service from Fatland Ford, carpets and mirrors and candlesticks, china and books and the microscope Audubon used in his work, Lucy's piano, and her husband's violin. The only thing left was the little cowhide trunk full of Audubon's drawings. Nobody wanted them.

Lucy and the two children had to stay with the Rankin family until Audubon was set free again.

"I'm such a failure," he told her when he had walked back to Henderson from the jail. "Thou would have been better off if thou had never met me."

"That I would not," said Lucy. "You are never a failure while you have your great talent. And we still have all your pictures."

Audubon smiled at his wife. "Let us look at the pictures," he said at last.

Together they opened the trunk. Then neither one could speak. A pair of Norway rats had built a nest for their young. To do it, they had chewed up two hundred drawings showing more than one thousand American birds.

This last blow stunned Audubon. For a while he did not eat. He could not sleep. But at last Lucy got him to drawing again. Once he made a start, back came his old ambition to make the new pictures perfect.

"There were lots of mistakes in those old ones," he told Lucy. "This time I will draw them better."

It would take years to fill the portfolio again. Meanwhile, he turned his hand to anything to feed his family. He drew portraits for five dollars, and sometimes much less. He painted the cabins of river steamboats. He even painted signs.

In the winter of 1819, the Audubons moved to the little city of Cincinnati in Ohio. There John James got a job stuffing birds and animals for a museum. But the museum could not pay the salary they had promised him, so Audubon decided to start a drawing school.

Only a few pupils came to the bare little house to learn drawing. Only one of them showed any real talent, and soon Audubon was devoting all his attention to thirteen-year-old Joe Mason. Joe knew a lot about plants, and he already painted them beautifully.

"What I'd like to do," Audubon told this boy, "is to paint all the birds in America, life size. How would you like to help me by putting in backgrounds in the pictures, flowers and branches and all?"

Joe looked at his teacher with eager eyes. "I would like nothing better in the whole wide world."

"We would have to do a lot of traveling," Audubon said, "all over the country, if we are to find every American bird."

Audubon told Lucy about it that night. "It is only a dream, thou sees. A bright dream that flies away like a bird."

"No, LaForêt," Lucy said. "This time your dream must come true. You have wasted too much time when you should have been doing only your real work. You will paint these birds, and then we shall get them published in books. You are going to be famous."

"But what about thee and my Kentucky Boys?" Audubon always called his two sons that.

"We shall be all right," Lucy insisted. "I can teach school here."

Lucy was determined now to let nothing stand in Audubon's way. She had an answer to every objection. In October, her husband and Joe Mason set out on a flatboat to paint birds all the way down the Ohio and Mississippi Rivers to New Orleans.

The crewmen of the flatboat were puzzled by all Audubon's drawing papers and crayons and watercolors which he kept dry and safe in the cabin. They could not see why a grown man should draw birds. But they admired his skill as a hunter and fisherman, for he kept them supplied with wild meat to pay his passage and Joe's.

Audubon and Joe walked in the woods every day, easily keeping pace with the slow flatboat. At sunset they brought back game to feed the crew and birds to paint. By the light of two candles in the cabin at night, and by dawnlight every morning, Audubon painted his birds. Joe put in the backgrounds. The pile of pictures grew.

By the time they reached the Missouri shores, Joe was almost as good a woodsman as Audubon. The two of them were ragged and dirty, but very happy. One day Joe grabbed Audubon's arm. He pointed to a treetop where a bald eagle sat. Audubon had not seen one since the day the Osages showed him his first Bird of Washington.

Very slowly he raised his rifle and took aim. It was not an easy shot, but the bird plunged to the ground. Audubon carried it in his arms to the boat. "I wish I did not have to kill him to paint him," he said.

For four whole days he painted the eagle. The cabin ceiling was so low that his head often ached because he had to sit hunched over his table. But he was proud of that picture. Lucy would be proud of it, too.

"Look!" Joe Mason said when the flatboat was pulling in at Natchez. Audubon saw him waggling the bare toes sticking out of his shoes. His own boots were just as bad.

"We'll take care of that," Audubon promised. He set out to look for a cobbler's shop.

"I am an artist," Audubon told the surprised cobbler. "Will you let me draw you and your wife for two pairs of stout boots?"

"Well, I don't rightly know," drawled the cobbler. "Leather costs money."

But in the end he and his wife were well pleased with their portraits. Joe and Audubon were just as happy with their new boots.

Audubon had almost no money in his pocket when they reached New Orleans. But he had a fine pile of bird pictures and a heart full of hope. People began gossiping about the ragged stranger who walked their town looking for work and talking about birds.

Audubon and Joe lived and ate and worked in one room. Sometimes they did not eat. But they made hunting trips into the forest and swamps. They brought back bright parakeets and even stranger birds. One day a hunter gave Audubon a snow-white egret he had found in the swamp.

"I'll have to buy a huge sheet of paper for this one," Audubon told Joe. "Every one of my birds must be exactly life size."

Lucy sent Audubon a parcel by steamboat. In it was a suit of fine clothes and his violin, which she had managed to buy back for him. What a difference those clothes made in the woodsman! Many New Orleans people were French, and they began gossiping more than ever.

"That monsieur is the very picture of an aristocrat...."

"I wonder who ...?"

"Do you suppose he *could* be the ...?"

Audubon never satisfied their curiosity. But sometimes he thought about his mysterious past and the promise he was keeping.

Now that he looked so much the fine gentleman, people were glad to have him teach their children French and drawing, dancing, and fencing. Boys were excited when they saw what a fine swordsman he was. Little girls were

Audubon lived and ate and worked in one room

charmed by his courtly manners and his gaiety. And they all liked the music he played on his fiddle.

One of his pupils was a young girl named Eliza Pirrie. When summer came, Eliza's mother invited Audubon to come to their plantation so she could go on with her lessons. She told him that he and Joe would live as members of the family. And the woods of Feliciana County teemed with birds.

Feliciana meant Happy Land, and it was a happy place for Audubon and Joe. They painted and roamed among the trees, under swinging Spanish moss. Audubon began planning to bring Lucy and his Kentucky Boys here. But in October, Eliza was taken ill. The doctor said there must be no more lessons for a long time. Audubon was given two hundred and forty dollars salary. It seemed like a fortune to him.

"I have rented a little house on Dauphine Street, my Lucy," he wrote when he got back to New Orleans. "I beg thee to join me there with our Kentucky Boys."

On the eighth of December, 1821, Lucy Audubon looked down from a high deck at her husband on the wharf. He was dressed in his best suit, and his brown curls were brushed to a high gloss.

"There's Papa!" shouted the two tall boys with her. Victor was twelve years old, and John was nine.

At Dauphine Street, Lucy did not start right in to put the untidy little house in order as most wives would. She went straight to the drawing board where her husband's portfolio lay. "I want to see every picture," she said.

Lucy did not hurry. She examined each drawing carefully. "They are the finest you have ever done, LaForêt," she said at last. "Soon we must see about getting them published."

"Minnie says you are a genius," Victor added. "Are you, Papa?"

Audubon's smile was a little crooked. "I can only hope Minnie is right," he said, looking at Lucy. "The good Lord knows I am not anything else."

The Feliciana money was soon gone. There was not much for the family on Dauphine Street to eat. Joe Mason told Audubon he was going back home to his family. He was tired of walking and working and never being sure he would not go hungry.

"You have your own future to think of," Audubon agreed. "I knew you would not stay with me forever."

He gave the boy his whole supply of drawing paper and chalks. He even made him a present of his best hunting rifle. Joe was very close to tears when he finally left. But he was proud, too, for Audubon had said he was sure Joe was going to become a famous painter and botanist.

Audubon began to feel depressed. He seemed as far away from fame as ever. But again Lucy encouraged him. She got work in a school where she could have the boys with her. Then she sent her husband out to explore and draw.

"I think I will go first to Natchez," Audubon said. "I hear there is an artist there named John Stein. He has been traveling in a wagon and doing portraits in oil paints. I want to see if he will teach me how to use oils."

Victor could not understand it. "But you are a wonderful painter already, Papa! Why do you want lessons from any other painter?"

"I do not know how to use oil colors, son. And I think a man is never too old to learn."

CHAPTER FIFTEEN

SUCCESS AT LAST

Captain Joseph Hatch, skipper of the packet *Delos*, sailing from New Orleans to Liverpool, was furious. It was bad enough to be becalmed in the Gulf of Mexico, but to see a man hanging by his feet from the bowsprit was more than he could bear.

"What does that fellow think he's doing?" he demanded.

"He says he wants to study the porpoises, sir," answered a grinning sailor. "They are playing follow-my-leader under our bow."

"Well, haul him aboard!" the captain ordered. "All I need now is to lose a passenger by some fool stunt like that!"

He was quite ready to lecture his foolhardy passenger, but John James Audubon gave him no opportunity.

"I was really quite safe, Captain," he said when the sailors had got him back on deck. "And I did want to get a close view of those fish. They are almost as graceful as birds. Perhaps you can tell me . . ."

Before he quite knew what was happening, Captain Hatch found himself answering all sorts of questions about fish and seabirds, especially birds. Then he was led to Audubon's stateroom to look at the contents of his portfolio. The captain whistled in surprise.

"I am taking the pictures to England in the hope of getting them published," Audubon told him. "But I regret that one picture is missing."

"Which is that?" the captain asked.

"The stormy petrel," Audubon said. Then he laughed. "I saw petrels twenty years ago when I came from France. The ship was stopped by a privateer. I almost lost my gold. We were nearly wrecked before reaching New York. Yet what I remember best is that I didn't dare ask the captain if I could use his dinghy. I wanted to get close to those petrels that rode the waves not far from us."

The captain turned over still another of Audubon's brilliant paintings. "Mr. Audubon, if the sea is calm, I will have my gig put overside for you at the first sign of a petrel."

Captain Hatch was as good as his word. On a calm day, John James bobbed up and down in the captain's gig, sketching the birds which paid no attention to him.

When he rowed back to the *Delos*, he was thinking of all the years that had led to this trip to England—and of Lucy, who had made the trip possible. Through all the hard times, she had never lost faith in him. She had gone on teaching in her own little school in West Feliciana. She had saved her earnings to send her wandering husband even farther away from her.

Audubon had journeyed up one river and down another, through trackless forests. He was always drawing birds, new birds by the hundreds.

"Sixteen and seventeen hours a day my husband works," Lucy had told people who thought him a lazy good-for-nothing. And she never felt sorry for herself.

Sometimes his boys had been able to travel with their father. John was showing a great deal of Audubon's talent for painting. Victor was working now in Louisville, in the counting house of Nicholas Berthoud. Mr. Berthoud was the son of the aristocratic old lady who had been lady-in-waiting to Queen Marie Antoinette. The Berthouds were still good friends of the Audubons, and Nicholas Berthoud had married Lucy's little sister, Eliza.

It was Lucy who had insisted one day that her husband was ready to show his work to the world. So he had bundled up his paintings and taken them to publishers in New York and Philadelphia. There he met nothing but discouragement. It was too expensive, all the publishers said, to engrave those pictures full size and then to color them by hand.

"It is hopeless, thou must see," Audubon had told Lucy when he returned to her little school in a mood of black despair.

"It is never hopeless while you have your hands and your eyes and your talent," she replied calmly. "Two more years of savings will take you to England. The best engravers in the world are there."

During those two years, Audubon had done some teaching himself in his wife's school. He had taught music and the elegant dances of old France. Then she had sent him away, and without shedding a tear, at least while he could see her.

Now here he was aboard a ship bound for England. As he watched the sailors haul in the captain's gig, he realized how much he owed to Lucy. It was her faith that had brought him so far. It was for her sake that he hoped for success in England. For her, he simply *had* to be successful.

He was successful! Not long after his arrival, doors were jammed at the galleries where his pictures were shown. Noblemen, artists, and scientists were glad to call themselves his friends. He made arrangements to have his pictures published in books, and the Queen of England ordered a set, though they would not be completed for several years and would cost more than a thousand dollars. He was feasted and made an honorary member of many learned societies.

He wrote to Lucy that it was Mr. Audubon here and Mr. Audubon there. He only hoped, he added, that they would not make a conceited fool out of Mr. Audubon in the end!

Now he could afford to send a golden brooch wrapped in the letter to Lucy, the best trinket he could buy her. Lucy loved it, but no more than she had loved a heron's feather or a wild columbine he had brought her when his pockets were empty.

Hints of the old mystery are in some of the letters Audubon intended only for Lucy's eyes. One day, he wrote her, the Countess of Selkirk visited him at his lodgings. And he wondered if the countess knew who he was positively, or whether she thought it was only John James Audubon, of Louisiana, to whom she spoke.

The Countess of Selkirk was the widow of a British nobleman who had helped aristocrats flee from France at the time of the French Revolution.

When he went to Paris, Audubon wrote another mysterious letter.

"It is a strange feeling to walk the streets of Paris after all these years, unknown and unnoticed, I who should command all! How often I have thought I might try to discover if my father is still in the memory of some I meet. And if... but if I say only a few words more, I must put an end to my existence, for I will have forfeited my word of honor and my oath."

What he meant, no one now can say. But he was wrong to say "unknown and unnoticed." For his pictures were as well received in France as they were in England, and his fame was as great. All that marred his triumph was that the Captain and Madame Audubon were no longer alive to share in his glory. They would have been so proud.

He threw his arms around the startled Englishman

SUCCESS AT LAST

All this time Audubon had been having difficulty finding the right engraver for his pictures. At last Mr. Robert Havell, the greatest engraver of his day, showed him the first completed picture, fully colored. Audubon stared in silence.

Then he threw his arms around the startled Englishman and danced him around the room in a rigadoon. All the time he was shouting, "The jig is up! The jig is up!"

"But, Mr. Audubon, what is the matter?" Mr. Havell asked.

"Matter? Why, it's perfect!"

John James Audubon's use of English was always rather original when he was excited.

By the time Audubon had been away from America for three years, he could not bear his homesickness. He wanted to see his wife and sons. And he missed his American birds.

On April 1, 1829, he sailed on the packet ship *Columbia*. He meant to go straight to Louisiana. But in Philadelphia someone told him about the birds in a great pine forest he had never visited and of other birds at Egg Harbor on the New Jersey coast. The temptation was too great. It was months before he reached Lucy. Lucy understood even that.

"But now we must never be apart, thee and I," Audubon told Lucy, as they walked at Feliciana the evening of his arrival.

Lucy smiled sadly. She knew better than to believe it. "At least, we must never be apart so long again, LaForêt."

CHAPTER SIXTEEN

MINNIE'S LAND

It was April of 1842, and John James and Lucy could smell spring in the air as soon as their carriage left the city. There was a film of green on the willow trees. The Hudson River glittered like a bright ribbon in the sunlight.

It was a trip far out into the country from the New York City of that day. But today, their destination would be right in New York, near 157th Street.

John James was taking his Lucy home at last.

There had been many more trips since he came back from England the first time: trips into the wilderness, sometimes alone, sometimes with his boys, and trips to England and back, when they had all gone together—Audubon and Lucy and both their sons. Victor had been good at handling business matters. John's talent in painting made him his father's assistant in new pictures.

John James Audubon now was a man famous on two

continents. The *Birds of America* had all been published, the greatest work on birds anyone had ever seen. There was a *Biography of Birds* completed now, too, with written descriptions of every picture in the big books called the elephant folios.

But Audubon had not given up working. He still spent many hours each day at his drawing board. He was doing the *Quadrupeds of North America*. As the carriage rumbled along the road, he told himself that he would like to paint every four-footed animal in the whole country.

At last the carriage turned in a long driveway, which led to a house overlooking the great river. It was set among tall elms and oak trees. Several tame fawns and an elk paid little attention to the carriage. They were used to it and to Audubon and his dogs. He had been there often during the past month, telling the workmen what to do and bringing furniture so that everything would be perfect for Lucy.

Lucy's eyes were shining as she walked onto the veranda and an apple-cheeked maidservant opened the door for her. But Audubon stopped his wife at the doorsill for a moment. He pulled an important-looking paper from his pocket and handed it to her with a very French bow.

"Whatever is it?" Lucy asked.

"It is the deed to *Minnie's Land*. It is all thine. The first place that is thy home, and *safe*, since I took thee away from Fatland Ford so many years ago."

"Any place I have lived with you has been home to me," Lucy said, looking up at him. "But I thank you for this, LaForêt."

"It is not a French palace," Audubon said, smiling. "But I think we will be happier here."

Was he thinking of the mystery in his life when he said this? If so, he promptly forgot it in the joy of showing Lucy her new home.

When she went into her parlor, Lucy could see that the place was already Audubon's. The mantelpiece was already crowded with stuffed birds. There were delightful drawings of field mice and woodpeckers and orioles everywhere. Together she and her husband looked at the pictures, remembering when each had been drawn, and where.

Two other carriages soon brought John and Victor with their wives and two rosy baby girls.

"This will be a fine place for our grandchildren," Audubon told Lucy. "The city is no fit place for anyone. There are so few birds!"

John had brought his portfolio. His father insisted on seeing his new picture right away. He studied it for a long time.

"With a son who can do as well as that," he said, "there is no need for the old man to work any longer. It is time I retired."

John and Victor both began to laugh. Audubon scowled. "You would mock your aged father, eh?"

"We're only remembering other times when you decided you were getting old," Victor said. "Two days after the first time, you were on your way to the Republic of Texas to visit President Houston in his Log Cabin White House. You explored Texas for three months, walking the whole way...."

"Yes," John said. "And don't forget the time he set out for Labrador in a raging storm. He had to visit some eider ducks up there."

"And that trip aboard the cutter *Marion* out among the Florida Keys..."

Audubon's face lit up. That Florida trip was one he liked to remember.

He had gone to Florida to study the great pink flamingos and had lived aboard the *Marion* for many days.

"I met a man on that trip who made up good songs," Audubon told his family. "He was German and a good man with a fiddle, too. I'd like to meet him again."

"There, you see," Lucy said. "You'll be off and away before we know it, LaForêt."

"No." Audubon sighed heavily. "I am really old now. Last week I was stiff after sleeping outdoors just one night in the woods."

"Didn't it rain that night?" John asked.

"Only a little bit. I'm getting on for sixty years old. It's really time I retired."

But Lucy did not believe that he was home for good. And of course she was right. Three weeks later, he was setting out on a long trip up the Yellowstone River. He was going right up to Canada, walking or paddling all the way.

There were still birds there he had not yet seen.

He had gone to Florida to study the great pink flamingoes

EPILOGUE

It is more than one hundred years since John James Audubon died at Minnie's Land. But people still argue about the mystery in his life. Books have been written claiming he was really the Dauphin Louis Charles who ought to have ruled France as King Louis XVII. This seems too good a story to be true, but we may yet learn once more that truth is stranger than fiction.

As Audubon himself would say, the important thing is not *who* he was but *what* he was. He fulfilled his great ambition to become the greatest painter of birds and the greatest authority on the birds of America. There are statues honoring him in cities where he once walked the streets without a penny in his pocket.

Nearly ten million boys and girls share his love of birds. They live in every state in the union and as far away as Australia. All of them explore the out-of-doors as Audubon himself did, with pencils and drawing paper. As he did, they study nature and the lives of the birds and animals. They have formed the Junior Clubs of the National Audubon Society. And that is the honor he would have liked most of all.

More Books from The Good and the Beautiful Library

Ladycake Farm
by Mabel Leigh Hunt

The Story of Edith Cavell
by Iris Vinton

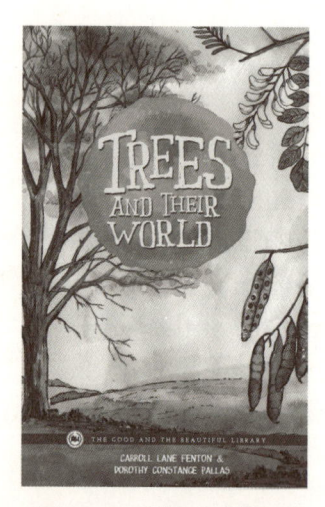

Trees and Their World
by C.L. Fenton & D.C. Pallas

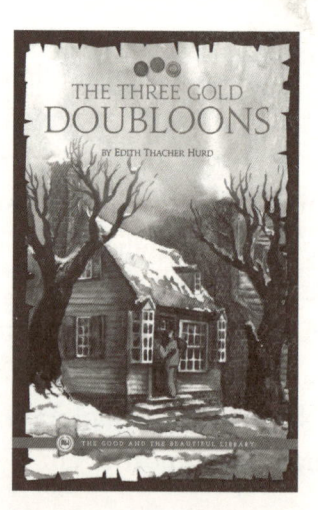

The Three Gold Doubloons
by Edith Thacher Hurd

goodandbeautiful.com